Choosing a Sustainable Future

CHOOSING A SUSTAINABLE FUTURE

The Report of the National Commission
on the Environment

ISLAND PRESS

Washington, D.C. □ *Corelo, California*

MEMBERS OF THE COMMISSION

CONTENTS

PREFACE

This report of the National Commission on the Environment is particularly timely as a new administration prepares to take office. There has been much solid progress in addressing environmental problems in the United States. If we are to address adequately the challenges of the future, however, it is time for basic change in environmental policy.

The National Commission on the Environment is a private-sector initiative convened by World Wildlife Fund (WWF), which provided funds and logistical support but has not sought in any way to influence this report.

The Commission's 19 members met 8 times—once in San Francisco, once in Racine, Wisconsin, and six times in Washington, D.C. The members are culturally, geographically, and occupationally diverse. They have expertise in government, science, economics, engineering, education, public policy, international finance, business, and religion; they come from both grassroots and national environmental organizations, and from federal and state environmental agencies. No person presently employed by government is included.

Despite the broad base of the Commission's membership, it has proved impossible to appoint individuals from all desirable areas without making the Commission unwieldy. We have tried to remedy these omissions by actively soliciting suggestions and comments from many groups and by briefing them on the progress of the Commission's work.

A remarkably high degree of agreement characterized the Commission's discussions, and all of the Commissioners subscribe to the basic themes of this report. In view of the large number of recommendations and the diverse composition of the Commission, it would have been remarkable if all the Commissioners had supported each of the recommendations, and in fact this was not the case. However, we are united behind the goal of sustainable development and fully support the basic approaches that the report recommends for achieving that goal.

The Commission recognizes that environmental issues are so broad in scope and touch on so many facets of American life that it would be impractical to try to deal with all of them in a single report, given the time constraints and resources available. The Commission has therefore been selective, focusing on those issues and concepts that appeared to us to have the highest priority. Moreover, because of the composition of this Commission, we focused more on the U.S. Environmental Protection Agency than on other environmental agencies.

We also limited our inquiry and recommendations to U.S. policy rather than proposing environmental policies for the world. Global policies and processes are urgently needed; nevertheless, our report focuses on U.S. policies that (necessarily in our view) affect both the domestic issues and international activities of our nation. Finally, we should note that the Commission has not undertaken original analysis but rather has drawn on the accumulated experience and wisdom of its members and of others.

Any introductory note of this kind would be incomplete without acknowledging the Commission's debt to J. Clarence (Terry) Davies, our executive director, and Amelia Salzman, our project director, without whose perseverance and energy this report might not have been written.

—RUSSELL E. TRAIN
Chairman
National Commission on the Environment

CRISIS AND OPPORTUNITY

We, the members of the National Commission on the Environment, are convinced that the natural processes that support life on Earth are increasingly at risk and that by choosing to act or not to act to confront this risk now, our country is choosing between two very different futures. If America continues down its current path, primarily reacting to environmental injuries and trying to repair them, the quality of our environment will continue to deteriorate, and eventually our economy will decline as well. If, however, our country pioneers new technologies, shifts its policies, makes bold economic changes, and embraces a new ethic of environmentally responsible behavior, it is far more likely that the coming years will bring a higher quality of life, a healthier environment, and a more vibrant economy for all Americans.

U.S. leadership should be based on the concept of *sustainable development*. By the close of the twentieth century, economic development and environmental protection must come together in a new synthesis: broad-based economic progress accomplished in a manner that protects and restores the quality of the natural environment, improves the quality of life for individuals, and broadens the prospects for future generations. This merging of economic and environmental goals in the concept of sustainable development can and should constitute a central guiding principle for national environmental and economic policymaking.

Sustainable development is predicated on the recognition that economic and environmental goals are inextricably linked. Long-term growth depends on a sound environment, and resources to protect the environment will come from economic strength. Both goals—that is, environmental and economic health—are intended to improve the quality of life of individuals, communities, and society. To the extent that either environmental or economic policy impoverishes the quality of life, it has failed.

The choice between crisis and sustainable development is one that our nation shares with the rest of the world. It must be addressed through international cooperation and by U.S. commitment to action at home and leadership abroad. As the world's single largest economy, the largest user of natural resources, the largest producer and consumer of energy, and the largest producer of carbon dioxide pollution, the United States has a special responsibility to exercise world leadership. Indeed, a commitment to such leadership is essential. The complexity and scope of current environmental challenges demand the ingenuity, expertise, and technology for which the United States is famous.

Over the past 20 years, an impressive array of federal, state, and local pollution control and resource management programs, both public and private, have been instituted in the United States. Total U.S. expenditures on environmental protection now average more than 2 percent of the gross national product annually. The United States has had the foresight to adopt stringent environmental laws and regulations and to make sizable economic investments in pollution control and energy efficiency. As a result, our nation has not had to contend with landscapes as blighted, air and water as polluted, soils as poisoned, or public health as ravaged as in Central and Eastern Europe. The measurable environmental progress made by the United States should be a source of national pride.

Still, our country's environmental achievements should not lull Americans into complacency. Despite numerous victories, the United States is losing many battles:

❖ *Global environmental problems* to which the United States makes no small contribution—loss of biodiversity, climate change, and stratospheric ozone depletion, for instance—are placing both human and natural systems at grave risk.

❖ The *air* in U.S. cities threatens to deteriorate further as improvements in auto emission controls are overwhelmed by the sheer numbers of cars and miles driven and by congestion. Meanwhile, indoor air pollution is largely ignored.

❖ Disposal and cleanup of the vast amounts of *waste* generated each year pose great difficulties and consume an increasing proportion of the limited funds available for environmental protection. Indirect sources of pollution, such as urban and agricultural runoff, continue almost unabated.

❖ Encroaching *land development* is displacing and undermining critical ecosystems such as wetlands and threatens rural landscapes, natural areas, and biological diversity.

❖ Large areas of national forest and other *public lands and resources* are not managed sustainably.

❖ *Farmlands* are suffering from soil loss and excessive use of chemicals.

❖ *Freshwater aquifers* are being consumed and contaminated at an alarming rate in many areas.

❖ *Overfishing and pollution* are seriously depleting our most important commercial fisheries.

❖ In many U.S. *inner cities*, the physical environment has the look of a wasteland.

This litany of environmental ills, familiar-sounding and by no means complete, is a product of today's level and character of economic activity and human population. We must also consider tomorrow. Over the next 50 years—within the lifetimes of many of us and of all our children—economic activity in the United States is projected to quadruple and global population to double at least. If growth of this magnitude occurs with current industrial processes, agricultural methods, and consumer practices, the results could be both environmentally and economically disastrous.

Forecasts based on linear projections are often wrong. In the case of environmental conditions, such projections may be too optimistic.

Ample evidence suggests that unless our nation acts decisively now, the price will be serious—in some instances irreversible—environmental harm. Undoubtedly, technology and manufacturing processes will evolve over the next 50 years, in some cases outstripping our imagination. However, in view of the fact that the versatile but polluting combustion engine is still with us, despite waves of technological innovation over the past century and our growing knowledge of how to bring alternatives on line, it would be the height of folly for our nation to sit back and simply hope that the future will be "greened" by an invisible hand. The United States must take deliberate steps to shape the future now.

Short-term needs are always more readily placed ahead of long-term goals and personal desires ahead of societal ones. Excuses for inaction—budget deficits, opposition to taxes, foreign competition—abound. Yet the continuing pursuit of "politics as usual" will almost certainly guarantee failure.

As history teaches, the only defense against political inertia is leadership, and in this regard environmental issues are no exception. The American public must insist that its leaders understand the stark realities of the environmental challenge. Leaders in business, government, labor, education, and the environmental community have to muster the political will to bring the nation together to face its problems head-on. Now more than ever, the American public has to become an informed, concerned, and committed public that will demand such leadership.

The United Nations Conference on Environment and Development, which met in Rio de Janeiro in June 1992, was an important beginning for the process of providing a new environmental agenda based on the concept of sustainable development. The need now is to translate that broad agenda into specific national action plans. Among other things, this report and the recommendations within it contain the ingredients of such a plan for the United States.

The course we chart will not be easy. Periodic adjustments will undoubtedly have to be made to minimize short-term economic and other difficulties. But there must be an end to U.S. ambivalence about the environment and a beginning of a steadfast commitment to improving the environment both nationally and internationally. *The United States must have a long-term strategy for pursuing the goal of sustainable development.* Such a balanced strategy should be able to anticipate and avoid severe local and regional economic dislocations and stimulate adjustment assistance and job retraining.

❖ ❖ ❖

As we stated at the outset, economic and environmental well-being are mutually reinforcing goals that must be pursued simultaneously if either is to be achieved. Economic growth cannot be sustained if it continues to undermine the healthy functioning of the Earth's natural systems or to exhaust natural resources. By the same token, only healthy economies can generate the resources necessary for investments in environmental protection.

Poverty is the enemy of the environment. Environmental protection is not possible where poverty is pervasive and the quality of life degraded. For this reason, one of the principal objectives of environmental policy must be to ensure a decent standard of living for all.

Innovations made to achieve sustainable development will themselves bring major economic benefits. The economic advantage of using materials and energy efficiently is obvious, and the domestic production and use of environmentally sound technologies will reap profits both for the U.S. firms that sell them and for those who use them.

The most efficient way to achieve environmental progress, therefore, is to harness market forces. Here, the role of public policy is to send the right signals to the economy—"getting the prices right" and making the marketplace work for instead of against environmental protection. Taxes and subsidies can be used to ensure that prices reflect environmental costs.

We harbor no illusions that market economics alone will put the United States or the world on the path to sustainable development. Government regulations and private and individual initiatives are also required. Regrettably, the U.S. statutory and regulatory system is woefully inadequate, cumbersome, and sometimes even perverse with respect to environmental issues. A regime that now emphasizes "end-of-the-pipe" cleanup must be radically reformed into one that makes use of economic incentives and encourages pollution prevention. Changing product design or manufacturing processes to minimize or prevent pollution is obviously superior to mandating expensive cleanups after the fact. And an environmentally literate public can encourage such efforts by demanding environmentally acceptable products.

If environmental prevention is to prevail over environmental cure and if the United States is to remain an international industrial leader, our country must rapidly develop and deploy a wide array of new, more efficient, and environmentally safe technologies. This need for new technology is particularly acute in the realms of transportation and energy generation because these activities currently account for so much environmental degradation.

Simply put, there must be a deep-seated change in how our country produces and uses energy. No single area of activity is so closely interwoven with the environment. Were it not for the world's large reliance on fossil fuels for both energy production and transportation, the problems of global warming, acid rain, and urban smog would be relatively minor. A progressive shift away from fossil fuels as quickly as possible in both the energy and transportation sectors is crucial. Because the United States uses in excess of one-fourth of the world's energy, largely generated by fossil fuels, it must be a leader in developing other energy sources.

Economic incentives dramatically different from those now in force are required. Coal, oil, and gas prices, for instance, must reflect the environmental costs associated with their combustion. Over the long term, the United States must shift to alternative nonpolluting sources of energy, principally from renewable sources. In the interim, the country must develop technologies that use energy more efficiently and thereby consume less fuel. A federal carbon tax should be phased in to move the economy in this direction and away from reliance on fossil fuels.

In transportation, the long-range need is a shift in auto technology to alternative sources of energy that will pollute our cities less. This will require incentives for more fuel-efficient autos and for fewer miles driven, as well as for new technologies such as electricity and, in the longer term, hydrogen. To curb current pollution levels, the federal gasoline tax should be raised gradually and predictably over several years—for example, by about $0.20 each year for five years. We believe that only an increase of this magnitude will work to change driving patterns and technological development. Even with this tax, the cost of gasoline in the United States would remain about the same price (in constant dollars) as the cost of premium gas here in 1981. Because of the potentially regressive impact of gasoline taxes, a system of tax credits or rebates could be used to offset hardships.

In agriculture, in manufacturing processes, in consumer products, and in almost every other sector of the economy, new technologies will give the United States a competitive edge as well as a healthier environment. The worldwide market for such technologies will continue to grow as the connections between environmental and economic well-being become more apparent. The economic potential of trade in such technologies is no secret; Japan and Germany, among others, have already moved aggressively into this field. If America moves ahead in this technology race, it will be because our country has at last understood that we need a technological revolution, not just another technical fix.

Along with dramatic economic opportunities, a commitment to sustainable development could bring timely new political opportunities, particularly in foreign affairs. With the end of the Cold War and the Communist threat, the bond that held the United States and its allies together for half a century has loosened. The international community is breaking into national or (at best) regional groupings pursuing their own narrow self-interests. Prospects for sustainable development could shatter in such a divided world. We are convinced that the urgent need to put the world on the road to sustainability provides a common purpose that can and must unite the global community.

While the principal thrust of this report is to recommend measures for putting America's environmental house in order, the United States has a huge stake in effectively addressing global environmental problems. As Barbara Ward and Rene Dubos said, all of us have two countries—"our own and Planet Earth." The threat of global climate change, for example, requires national initiatives in the United States, but the problem really can be addressed only through a common worldwide effort. The destruction of forests will exacerbate global warming and accelerate the loss of species and ecosystems, foreclosing medical, recreational, and trade opportunities for the United States as well as diminishing the world's shared biological heritage. The great potential for expanding trade with developing countries will not be realized unless these nations achieve sustainable development. U.S. national security interests depend increasingly on achieving a level of international stability that can come only from sustainable development.

The most critical need facing the world is the control of human numbers. Continued global population growth of the current magnitude—one billion more people every decade—will swamp economic and social progress as well as efforts to protect the environment. Our nation and all others will gain from efforts to stabilize world population and to improve living standards in developing countries, where 90 percent of the projected population growth will occur. The burden placed on the environment is a product of population and consumption. The priorities for the developed countries are to switch to sustainable technologies and to reduce wasteful consumption; the priorities for the developing countries are to develop sustainably and curb population growth.

The United States must make a major commitment to cooperate with the world community to stabilize global population, recognizing the linkages between birth rates, child survival, economic development, education, and the economic and social status of women. Universal access to effective family-planning information, contraceptives, and health care is essential. We recommend a reversal of the U.S. policy that prohibits funding to certain family-planning organizations, and we urge greatly increasing U.S. funding of international population programs and of economic assistance to developing countries.

A key failure in the U.S. effort to address environmental needs has been the widespread failure to recognize the need for effective land-use planning. We do not suggest that the federal government should preempt the traditional roles of state and local governments in this area. The federal government must lead the way by managing its own lands consistent with the principle of sustainable development. State and local governments as well as other regional groups should undertake land-use planning for a variety of reasons: to protect environmentally sensitive areas, including watersheds, aquifers, and wetlands; to maintain biological diversity; to sustain the productivity of agricultural land; to ensure that sites for economic activity are appropriate and available; to encourage energy efficiency; and to protect sites of natural beauty and of historic and cultural value. To help make land use consistent with the overarching goal of sustainable development, we recommend the enactment of federal legislation that encourages state and regional authorities to develop land-use planning procedures based on such criteria.

Sustainable development depends on integrating environmental values into policy and decisionmaking across an entire spectrum of governmental functions. To facilitate integration as well as the major changes in current environmental policies that we envision, a cabinet-level Department of the Environment is needed—not just an elevated Environmental Protection Agency, but a department with additional functions and roles. This department cannot be exclusively or primarily regulatory but must also be able to formulate and oversee the implementation of a National Environmental Strategy. It can spearhead a radical revision of our country's pollution control laws to encourage innovation, pollution prevention, and more coherent, cross-media approaches. The President and Congress should be united on such a goal and on the overall national and global strategy.

As human population inevitably will continue to increase for the next half-century or more, and as sustainable development will not be an easy accomplishment, citizens must learn to devote themselves to the achievement of long-term goals, not just short-term satisfactions. The nation must stop stealing the environmental capital of future generations and must live instead on its fair share of nature's interest.

An informed citizenry with an ethical commitment to care for the environment is essential to the future we envision. Success with the technological, economic, and governmental changes that we recommend is predicated on the understanding and wholehearted support of the American people. Environmental values must be integrated into the lifestyles of individuals and families as well as into the conduct of businesses, labor, and governments.

To this end, the nation as a whole and especially its schools must pledge themselves to the goal of environmental literacy. U.S. citizens must have the knowledge, practical competence, and moral understanding to cooperate in building a sustainable civilization. The pursuit of environmental literacy will require curricular innovations from kindergarten through college, changes in teacher education programs, expanded graduate programs, and continuing education, both formal and informal. Enhanced science research will improve our knowledge of ecosystems, habitats, and public health and will add to environmental literacy.

All of us must develop a greater sense of ethical responsibility for the environment. Environmental ethics are founded on an awareness that humanity is part of nature and that nature's myriad parts are interdependent. In any natural community, the well-being of the individual and of each species is tied to the well-being of the whole. In a world increasingly without environmental borders, each individual and every nation has a fundamental ethical responsibility to respect nature and to care for the Earth, protecting its life-support systems, biodiversity, and beauty. In this extraordinarily interdependent world, each person should feel an ethical responsibility not only to a local or national community but to the larger global community and to future generations.

It is only within such a framework that the values to sustain and guide us will be found as we move toward the goal of sustainable development. Schools, religious institutions, and the news media as well as businesses, governments, and (perhaps above all) families must share in the tasks of achieving this aim.

We have a vision for the future: a vision of an America and a world in which humanity lives and prospers in harmonious, sustainable balance with the natural systems of the Earth. America has an opportunity to rise to the challenge of environmental leadership as it has to the causes of human liberty, equality, and free and open markets. The challenge starts at home.

This introductory statement summarizes the main focuses of the Commission's thinking as well as its principal recommendations. Detailed discussion and additional recommendations are found in the full report.

KEY
RECOMMENDATIONS

Chapter 1. The Goal of Sustainable Development: Sustainable development should be the primary goal of environmental and economic policy.

Chapter 2. Technologies for Sustainable Development: The most important and immediate target of U.S. environmental policy is to encourage the development and adoption of technologies compatible with sustainable development.

Design for the environment must take its place alongside cost, safety, and health as a guiding criterion for technology development. It is imperative that the government provide incentives for the development and adoption of environmentally benign technologies.

New federal tax and other policies, such as enactment of a carefully crafted investment tax credit or "green" research and development tax incentives, are needed to stimulate savings and investment in environmentally advantageous technologies.

In the discharge of their responsibilities, especially in procurement decisions, government agencies must make deliberate efforts to encourage new technologies.

The United States should promote a business climate to help U.S. environmental technology companies compete in the growing world market and should stimulate the global market for new technologies. It should also launch a coordinated international research effort to develop environmentally sound technologies.

The federal government should substantially increase funding for research and development, and participate in partnerships with private industry to explore new and innovative technologies that are environmentally sound.

Regulations affecting technology should be based on extensive and unbiased assessments of the technological possibilities and associated costs as well as their effectiveness in promoting technology development and use. Regulatory obstacles to the development and introduction of environmentally superior technology should be removed.

Chapter 3. Economics for Sustainable Development: Getting the prices right involves eliminating price-distorting subsidies, taxing environmentally harmful activities, and revising the way economic activity is measured.

The federal tax on gasoline should be increased gradually and predictably over several years—for example, by $0.20/gallon annually for five years.

The United States should enact a carbon tax phased in over several years—for example, starting at $6/ton of carbon and increasing over five years to $30/ton.

Water subsidies to growers should be reduced or eliminated.

Resource and environmental factors should be incorporated into macroeconomic measures.

Chapter 4. Environmental Literacy: Schools, families, religious institutions, the media, businesses, and government must cooperate in fostering the development of an environmentally literate citizenry that respects environmental values and assumes responsibility for putting the values into practice.

State and local governments should continue to develop and institute interdisciplinary environmental curricula. The federal government should provide resources, including financial support, for the development and implementation of state and local environmental-education initiatives.

Corporate leaders should make long-term environmental management a basic component of their strategic decisionmaking and planning.

Businesses should undertake regular environmental audits and make periodic reports to the public on their environmental performance.

Consumer-labeling efforts should continue to involve government, private industry, consumer groups, and environmental organizations in developing labels that are clear and easily understood by the consumer.

Chapter 5. Governance for Sustainable Development: Environmental considerations must become integral to all governmental policies.

Congress and the President should work together to develop a National Environmental Strategy. This strategy should be the basis for federal agencies to incorporate environmental considerations into their plans and policies. It should also be the basis for the federal government's work with the private sector to achieve sustainable development.

Congress must reform its committee structure to avoid overlap and confusion over environmental issues.

Congress and the President should create a Department of the Environment. A principal function of the new department would be the formulation and oversight of the National Environmental Strategy.

The Council on Environmental Quality (CEQ) should be strengthened and revitalized.

Regaining trust should be a goal of every government agency and employee and of every political reformer and policymaker.

Congress should pass legislation clearly waiving federal immunity from the application and enforcement of federal environmental laws.

The U.S. Environmental Protection Agency (EPA) should give higher priority to environmental equity and revise its data collection, assessment, and citizen participation efforts accordingly.

Chapter 6. America's New Global Role: The United States has a vital interest in leading efforts to protect the global environment, moderate world population growth, and improve the standard of living in developing nations.

The United States should make protecting the global environment a high-priority concern of both domestic and foreign policy.

Concluding effective international environmental agreements should become a higher priority of the United States. Specifically, the United States should sign the biodiversity treaty and aggressively implement and strengthen the climate convention, reevaluating the convention's terms as the science evolves.

The United States should actively promote the effective implementation of Agenda 21 and support both a strong Commission on Sustainable Development to follow up on the Earth Summit and a new U.N. environmental agency, built out of the United Nations Environment Programme (UNEP), to promote international environmental cooperation and agreement.

The U.S. development assistance program and other U.S. policies affecting developing countries should be reoriented and enhanced to achieve sustainable development and to protect the global environment.

The United States should sharply increase its overall financial support for development assistance to developing countries.

The U.S. Foreign Assistance Act should be rewritten to address the environmental and development challenges of the post-Cold War era, and the U.S. Agency for International Development should be strengthened and revitalized to give development assistance a fresh start.

An international system of regional centers, including existing national and regional centers and institutions, should be established to develop, disseminate, and encourage the use of environmentally sustainable technologies.

The United States should urge the former Eastern bloc nations to incorporate environmental considerations into their economic reforms and should provide technical assistance to implement such measures.

To meet its proportionate share of the U.N. goal, the United States should increase its population assistance to at least $650 million in 1993 and to at least $1.2 billion in 2000.

The United States should demonstrate its leadership in meeting the demand for population-related services by increasing its assistance to developing countries for population programs and services and by reversing its "Mexico City Policy."

The United States should provide leadership in promoting the rights and status of women worldwide.

The United States should support free trade, with safeguards to ensure that all countries move toward high environmental standards.

The United States, in consultation with interested parties, should formulate and urge adoption of GATT provisions that prevent trade rules from undermining environmental measures and that also prevent spurious environmental measures from being used as trade barriers.

Chapter 7. Energy and the Environment: The most critical technologies for sustainable development are energy technologies. Highest priority should go to energy efficiency.

The states and the federal government should develop and maintain programs that provide incentives for energy efficiency, such as allowing utilities to earn as much by improving efficiency as by increasing production.

The Department of Energy's R&D budget should be reoriented to emphasize renewable and nonfossil fuel sources of energy.

Implementing the gasoline and carbon taxes recommended in Chapter 3 would contribute significantly to putting America on an energy path consistent with sustainable development.

Chapter 8. Preventing Pollution: Efforts to halt pollution should become more integrated and holistic; pollution prevention should take priority over pollution control.

The Toxics Release Inventory (TRI) provisions should be expanded to cover more types of industries and more facilities, including federal facilities. The TRI should be combined with facility planning to reduce toxics.

Congress should enact legislation requiring the new Department of the Environment to begin issuing integrated permits covering air, water, and solid waste by 1997. Working with Congress, the Department should develop legislation for integrating all pollution control functions as soon as is practicable.

The government should give high priority to efforts to narrow the gap between public perceptions of risk and expert evaluations of risk. These efforts should include promoting citizen participation.

EPA or the Department of the Environment should establish an office for long-range forecasting, and CEQ, working closely with state and federal environmental agencies, should issue periodic reports articulating 5- and 10-year environmental quality goals with specific and measurable national, state, and international objectives.

A Center for Environmental Statistics should be established in the Department of the Environment. The center, working closely with CEQ and other agencies, should produce regular reports on environmental conditions and trends.

Chapter 9. Habitats for Humans and Other Species: Environmentally sensitive management of public and private land is essential to achieving environmental goals and economic growth over the long term.

Congress should enact legislation to:
— support state and local land-use planning by identifying and establishing planning criteria to provide for balanced use of lands, to protect environmental quality, and to provide for economic and other social purposes; and
— ensure that any federal actions are consistent with and meet state or local plans that accord with the federal criteria, and provide financial support for development and implementation of the state plans.

Management on public lands that is now based on multiple use should be made compatible with sustainability.

The President should issue an executive order establishing an interagency policy committee on federal lands to identify and to establish priorities and coordinate the management of environmentally significant federal lands.

Subsidies and below-market arrangements that encourage unsustainable use of natural resources on public lands should be eliminated.

Protection and enhancement of the native biodiversity and important ecosystems of the United States should be a national goal, and the federal government should institute a national policy strategy aimed at conserving biodiversity.

Congress should enact legislation requiring a National Inventory of Biodiversity for public and private lands and establishing a mechanism for disseminating this information to planners and resource managers.

Congress should increase appropriations for the Endangered Species Act with particular support for Habitat Conservation Plans.

The Magnuson Act should be significantly amended to provide better long-term protection for commercial fish species.

CHAPTER ONE

THE GOAL OF SUSTAINABLE DEVELOPMENT

**We envision an America in which public and private values
and actions promote sustainable development.**

❖

**Sustainable development should be the primary goal
of environmental and economic policy.**

Sustainable development represents a new synthesis of economic development and environmental protection. It offers a central principle for national environmental and economic policymaking and for environmental management.

Simply put, the United States has a vital interest in achieving and maintaining a healthy environment to (among other things) support economic development on a long-term basis. It also has a vital interest in pursuing economic growth that will protect and restore the environment over the long run. The result of combining these two goals is sustainable development. It is the recognition that neither environmental health nor economic prosperity is viable without the other.

Although both economic growth and environmental improvement are now accepted national goals, this was not always the case. Until recently, industrial development occurred with little regard for environmental protection, and the cost of correcting the resulting environmental damage has been far higher than the cost of preventing the damage would have been.

The remarkable burgeoning of environmental laws in the 1970s and 1980s underscored the American people's determination to safeguard the environment. An important development from those years is the recognition that the economy and the environment are neither separate nor necessarily in conflict over the long term; rather, they are mutually dependent. *The challenge now is to infuse government, corporate, and individual decisionmaking with an awareness of the importance of sustainable development.*

THE CONCEPT OF SUSTAINABLE DEVELOPMENT

Sustainable development is a strategy for improving the quality of life while preserving the environmental potential for the future, of living off interest rather than consuming natural capital. Sustainable development mandates that the present generation must not narrow the choices of future generations but must strive to expand them by passing on an environment and an accumulation of resources that will allow its children to live at least as well as, and preferably better than, people today. Sustainable development is premised on living within the Earth's means.

The key element of sustainable development is the recognition that economic and environmental goals are inextricably linked. Long-term growth depends on a sound environment, and resources to protect the environment will be forthcoming only from a strong economy. Both goals are intended to improve the quality of life of individuals, communities, and society. To the extent that either environmental or economic policy impoverishes the quality of life, it has failed. The protection of parks, wetlands, and wilderness areas contributes to the quality of life and is an essential element of environmental policy. Similarly, ensuring that every individual has adequate food, clothing, and shelter is a basic part of economic policy.

Sustainable development does not mean leaving all of nature cordoned off and untouchable, just as it does not mean developing every acre. Sustainable development has as its goal a decent standard of living for all, coupled with maintenance of the integrity of all environmental systems. It means employing some natural resources for human use but replenishing them either directly with the same kind of resource, or indirectly with a substitute—but only after careful consideration of its effect on the ecosystem. (Society uses coal to generate electricity, for example, but it is confident that future generations will have substitute fuels. It is searching for substitutes for coal because of the adverse effects of fossil fuels on ecosystems.)

Sustainable development also means using resources reasonably and efficiently. It means approaching development in a way that examines environmental implications up front and accounts for them. It means preventing pollution in the first instance.

Managing economic and environmental resources together is integral to sustainable development. *To avoid wasting time and money, the national environmental agenda should focus on problems that are bona fide priorities.* Legislators and regulators should direct their efforts toward the most important problems in the most cost-effective ways. Industry should have clear incentives to innovate, leap-frogging obsolete approaches to be as environmentally sound and as competitive as possible in the global marketplace. In short, the public has a right to protection of the environment in a way that makes the best use of natural and economic resources in all phases of policymaking.

Pressures on the planet are enormous. The increase in world population in the next decade alone will equal the entire world population in 1800. The increase in the gross domestic product (GDP) of the United States in a typical year today exceeds the total GDP of the world in 1900. New technologies are being developed at a geometrically increasing rate; each year brings more technologies that will accelerate the rate of change.

In this resource-intensive situation, sustainability must be a guide toward patterns of growth that maintain the integrity of the environmental base. The numerous interpretations of sustainability do not undermine its importance or usefulness. Every major concept that encompasses human ideals, such as liberty, democracy, and self-fulfillment, is subject to diverse meanings. A concept that is broad in scope, large in effect, and significant in its embodiment of human values cannot help but be subject to some ambiguity. Indeed, these characteristics are necessary for the concept to remain a fundamental tenet that can guide human decisions for generations to come.

However, despite the pathbreaking work of the World Commission on Environment and Development, some people consider the concept of sustainable development not only ambiguous but a contradiction. For them, development implies economic growth, which they find to be fundamentally antagonistic to environmental protection. This is one of several false assumptions that must be abandoned if environmental policy is to move toward the future envisioned by this Commission.

Much of the environmental policy debate over the past several decades has centered on a series of choices between what have been perceived as conflicting goals and values: whether the best approach to environmental protection is to influence people's behavior or to encourage new technology; whether achieving environmental quality is compatible with economic growth; whether the needs of humankind should take priority over the protection of nature; or whether U.S. interests are compatible with global interests.

We recognize that choices have to be made and that there is some real basis for each of these dichotomies. However, we also believe in a synthesis based on sustainability.

Behavior and Technology. Should society rely on technology or behavioral changes to protect the environment? There is skepticism in certain quarters about the notion of technology solving environmental problems. Until the Industrial Revolution and the beginning of the technological age, humans lacked the capacity to do major damage to global systems. To be sure, natural resource abuses by earlier civilizations contributed to their decline. But nothing compares with the actual or potential destructiveness of some forms of modern technology. Even with the best intentions, newly adopted technologies can have unanticipated and often adverse consequences, and technology assessment has not been particularly successful in preventing negative effects. For example, liquids used for refrigeration and thought to be inert turn out to destroy the stratospheric ozone layer; fire retardants used on such items as children's clothes are linked to possible cancer risk. Putting faith in technology, critics say, will lead to disappointment.

However, lifestyle change is a difficult, time-consuming, and uncertain proposition. Examples of lifestyle changes in the United States include reduced cigarette smoking, more recycling, and the wearing of seat belts. These changes have occurred as a result of a combination of approaches ranging from education to regulation. Despite greater awareness of the importance of protecting the environment, most people in both industrialized and developing countries want the benefits that technology can bring—and they want more of these benefits, not fewer. Meanwhile, continuing and increasing environmental problems result from the pace of demand for resources and energy. The

United States has historically been the world leader in technology development. American technological ingenuity has rapidly responded to changing demands.

In the long run, changes in values and in technology are equally necessary and complementary. And, technology and lifestyle are linked. Attitudes toward technological change will have a major effect on the type and rate of technologies adopted. Some new technologies will foster new attitudes and behavior with respect to the environment. New energy-efficient technologies, for example, can both save money and benefit the environment.

Major efforts are needed to educate people about the environment and to instill in each person a respect for nature and a recognition of humanity's dependence on it. This report outlines a series of recommendations to help create an environmentally literate society. Simultaneously, new environmentally sensitive technologies must rapidly be developed and adopted, and existing technologies must be more widely used to sustain the Earth's resources. A new generation of more environmentally benign technologies are needed in energy, agriculture, manufacturing, and all other sectors.

Economic Growth and Environmental Quality. How much truth is there to the perceived tradeoff between economic gain and improved environmental quality? There is no question that environmental protection requires economic resources, whether that means investing resources in pollution control equipment or losing land for buildings by protecting a wetland or coastal area. However, there are two significant reasons why the choice between economic growth and environmental quality is usually false.

First, there is ample evidence that greater environmental protection is often better for the economy. Economic growth based on the destruction of natural resources and deterioration of environmental quality is not sustainable, whether in the United States or in developing nations. Using up natural resources can erode the base for future economic development and ecological support. In countries such as Haiti, overuse and exhaustion of resources have crippled the economy, resulting in still more overuse of what little remains of the natural resource base. In some Central and Eastern European countries, the air, water, and soil have been so poisoned with the toxic by-products of manufacturing that sickness and chronic health problems are damaging the economy.

Second, the choice between economic growth and environmental protection is usually false because it does not account for the quality of life. Traditionally, economic growth has been the measure of improvements in the material aspects of life. Yet there is usually a difference between greater economic growth (especially as currently measured nationally; see Chapter 3) and a better quality of life for individuals. Although economic growth is imperative for developed and developing countries, many individuals would choose cleaner water over an increase in the gross domestic product or even over an increase in personal salary. For this reason, economic growth is a poor proxy for long-term improvements in the quality of life.

The question whether nature imposes limits to economic growth is centuries old. In the very long run, of course, nothing can grow indefinitely. In the very short run, economic growth can occur even under the most adverse environmental conditions. The more useful question is whether the environment limits growth over a period that is relevant for current policymaking—within the next century.

Physical limits to growth could become all too apparent if new policies are not adopted. For example, the atmosphere has a limited capacity to absorb carbon dioxide emissions before the Earth's temperature will rise. If there were no way for economic development to occur without generating additional carbon dioxide, then global warming could form an absolute limit to growth. However, many existing technologies produce energy with lower carbon dioxide emissions. If these alternative technologies were to be widely adopted, global warming would probably not pose an absolute limit to economic growth. The recommendations in this report are intended to prevent what we perceive as potential limits to growth from becoming actual limits.

Humanity and Nature. The conflict between human beings and nature is another ancient theme that has taken on new meaning as humanity's power over nature has increased. Nature used to be Goliath and humankind, David. The roles are now reversed, and people are inflicting major damage on the natural world. Are humans and nature bound to be locked in conflict?

Moving beyond this theme makes sense—has long made sense—for both pragmatic and ethical reasons. Pragmatically, society is rediscovering how dependent it is on natural systems. People cannot escape the need to keep their natural surroundings functional. Ethically, more and more people are recognizing that each person is part of a larger community that includes the natural world. Societies are realizing that humanity and nature are not opponents but should coexist as integral parts of a larger whole. Increasingly, moral and religious leaders are espousing reverence and respect for nature rather than championing human dominion over it.

The United States and the World. Can the United States formulate policy in isolation from the rest of the world? A new recognition of the collective interests of all nations is emerging. Drug problems in U.S. cities are related to activities in Asia and Latin America. Wall Street brokers start the day by listening to London and Tokyo. The marketplace is ever more linked; as are the effects of pollution and the responsibility and ability to remedy them. Solutions to global environmental threats require the active cooperation of all nations.

In the past, resource use and pollution were largely a concern of each individual country. Today, because of improved science, technology, awareness, and communications, people are learning that the decisions of individual countries can harm the global commons. Thus, a small number of countries can endanger a resource essential to the entire world, such as the stratospheric ozone layer. Environmental pressures in other parts of the world can affect the industrial growth options and standards of living at home.

With the growing awareness of the implications of each nation acting in isolation, new political splits and tensions are emerging; so, too, are new international agreements, organizations, and instruments. To maintain political and environmental security in these circumstances, the world's nations must recognize their mutual dependence on the Earth's resources and share responsibility for them. At home and abroad, the United States must be a leading force in forging and strengthening partnerships and arrangements to achieve sustainable development.

This will require charting a new course in the United States, where international policies in such specific areas as the environment often develop on an ad hoc basis with insufficient preparation, confused responsibilities, and a general sense that what the rest of the world thinks or does is not very important. Shortsightedness with regard to global environmental issues will be increasingly costly because this country cannot restore or maintain its environment apart from the rest of the world.

The United States must move beyond its preoccupation with these old conflicts. They interfere with a realistic understanding of the present world and impede policy reforms urgently needed to cope with environmental threats. *Far-reaching new policies are needed to deal with the potentially devastating combination of explosive population growth, unprecedented economic expansion, and harmful side effects from industrial technologies and overconsumption.*

As currently formulated, U.S. policies are proving inadequate to solve many of today's problems, much less cope with new ones. Indoor air pollution, many kinds of habitat threats, and water pollution from nonpoint sources such as urban and agricultural runoff go largely neglected. Management of public lands succeeds only in antagonizing those who would use such lands for economic gain, on the one hand, and those who would preserve them for recreation and aesthetic enjoyment, on the other. In the meantime, environmental quality suffers and declines.

The environmental statutes and regulatory strategies of the previous decades have contributed significantly to environmental protection. But as our understanding of environmental threats and regulatory limits has improved, the shortcomings of these approaches have become ever more apparent. Many of the statutory provisions and implementing regulations are antiquated, cumbersome, counterproductive, and even incomprehensible. *Comprehensive reform is imperative to refocus the regulatory system on coherent policies that can bring about sustainable development, encourage environmentally benign technologies, and institute effective incentives for innovation and behavioral change.*

In a world where global environmental problems now number among the greatest threats to national security, reconciling old conflicts will position the United States to lead in adopting the policies necessary for a sustainable future. We recognize that most political processes continue to emphasize short-term rather than long-term considerations. Many of the most volatile environmental conflicts, in fact, are conflicts between the short term and long term: preserving loggers' jobs now versus developing a forest industry that is sustainable over the long term; confronting political and economic crises as they arise in developing countries versus assisting those countries now to avoid crises in the future; risking a world population that will strain sustainability to or beyond its limits versus moderating population growth.

To frame debates over the protection of species or global warming purely in the context of the current job market reflects either a misunderstanding of the significance of the issues or a disregard for the long-term interests of the United States. It plays upon the understandable fears of those whose jobs may be at risk or who fear they may otherwise be disadvantaged.

The United States can no longer afford or accept politics or economic analyses in which the emphasis is exclusively short term. What is needed is a long-term vision that positively meshes environmental quality with economic strength. *A strategy to realize that vision must be balanced to anticipate and mitigate economic dislocations through job retraining and new economic opportunities that will arise from the development of new, clean technologies and their diffusion in the global marketplace.*

Today, issues such as world deforestation, global climate change, depletion of fishery stocks, and loss of biological diversity, habitats, and soils go to the heart of the Earth's support system and thus to human survival. They underpin job creation and sustainable economic activity in the long term. The first step in dealing with these issues is to develop and adopt a new generation of environmentally compatible technologies—the topic of the next chapter of our report.

CHAPTER TWO

TECHNOLOGIES FOR SUSTAINABLE DEVELOPMENT

We envision an America in which a new generation of technologies contributes to the conservation of resources and the protection of the environment.

✤

The most important and immediate target of U.S. environmental policy is to encourage the development and adoption of technologies compatible with sustainable development.

The current trajectory of technology development will lead to eventual deterioration of the natural environment and the quality of human life. A new generation of technologies designed from the start to minimize stress on the environment is needed in all fields—transportation, agriculture, manufacturing, and energy use and production.

Technology is a broad term that applies to the techniques for making useful things and that encompasses the processes, procedures, and methods by which people make and use them. Tractors, television sets, and aircraft are products of technology, as are systems of crop irrigation and airline reservations. Humans have used technology to adjust to, protect themselves from, and exploit the environment. The application of technology has been the central means of greater human productivity and consequent increases in standards of living. It has also provided humankind with tremendous environmental benefits, such as sanitary water supply systems, relief from disease, and enhanced industrial safety. However, as technology has increased in sophistication and

11

complexity, so have its adverse and widespread impacts on the environment. Poor agricultural practices have devastated soils; plastic packaging has complicated the disposal of solid wastes; and the increased production of electricity from fossil fuels has resulted in rising emissions of carbon dioxide that threaten the climate.

Sensitive use of technology offers hope of ameliorating environmental degradation; insensitive use guarantees the opposite. Society has a choice. Technology can be a key to a sustainable world, or it can be a major impediment.

CHARACTERISTICS OF THE NEW TECHNOLOGY

Sustainable development requires a new technological ethic—a new set of values that will shape the development and adoption of superior technologies. Technology in the future must be designed to minimize undesirable effluents, emissions, and wastes from products and processes. The new technological ethic espouses "closed" technological systems that produce the least waste and use the fewest resources.

Technology for sustainable development must focus on pollution prevention (see Chapter 8). This requires a total systems approach that prevents pollutants from being created in the first place or minimizes undesirable wastes and obviates the need for many controls. A preventive approach involves using fewer or nonpolluting materials, designing processes that minimize pollutants or that direct them to other useful purposes, and creating recyclable products. The preventive/systems approach requires examining the full life-cycle of products and practices.

Minimizing the volume of materials used is another characteristic of the new technological ethic. Technology has historically moved in the direction of dematerialization, which can benefit the environment. Optical fibers have replaced copper wires for communications, silicon chips have replaced vacuum tubes for electronic uses, composite materials have replaced metals in many applications because of weight and strength advantages. These and other technological substitutions have increasingly reduced the volume of materials needed to perform industrial, agricultural, and other societal functions, thereby reducing the amount of natural materials used.

The first target of new technologies in the United States must be energy use and production (see Chapter 7). Fossil fuels, the dominant source of energy supply sustaining modern civilization, create some of the most threatening environmental problems, ranging from global-scale changes in climate to regional effects of acid deposition to local urban air pollution problems and health and safety risks in mining and production. Environmental concerns and U.S. dependence on foreign sources of fuel require the development of technologies that increase the efficiency of energy production and end use and the further development and use of alternative energy technologies based on nonfossil fuels.

Finally, both industry and the government must assess the effectiveness of new technologies in meeting the goals of pollution prevention, waste minimization, and economic efficiency to ensure that any new technology is an environmentally superior technology.

OBSTACLES TO THE ADOPTION OF ENVIRONMENTALLY SUPERIOR TECHNOLOGIES

Despite the need for (and, in many cases, availability of) new and superior technologies, many obstacles presently exist that prevent their widespread use. An environmentally superior technology may not be used because it is not commercially viable (i.e., because it is more expensive than competing technologies); because its existence is not widely known among potential users; or because there are regulatory, cultural, or institutional barriers to its adoption.

The limited use of integrated pest management (IPM) techniques in agriculture illustrates this problem. In some cases, IPM is not used because farmers believe (usually erroneously) that it would be more expensive than routine application of chemical pesticides or that IPM would result in lower crop yields. In other instances, farmers and state extension agents may not know about IPM methods or may be reluctant to use or recommend new and unfamiliar methods.

Similarly, there are known technologies that can reduce energy demand, reduce the contaminating effects of fossil fuel emissions, or reduce the use of toxic materials. For example, alternatives to many chlorofluorocarbon (CFC) applications, such as in solvents, blowing agents, and refrigeration, are available; however, economic and political obstacles have hindered their rapid diffusion into the economies of both developing and developed countries.

Investment in the Status Quo. A principal roadblock to the introduction of technological improvements that have environmental benefits is the economic investment in existing technologies. For example, individuals do not want to buy new cars sooner than necessary, and manufacturers resist making major changes in production machinery unless it will be profitable. Manufacturers are reluctant to abandon the long years of experience and considerable expertise invested in and gained from existing technology.

Pricing. Another roadblock is the failure of the economy to incorporate environmental damage and other "externalities" into the cost of products. As discussed in Chapter 3, in a free market, if the price of a technology reflects societal as well as private costs, society will quite literally buy the amount of environmental protection it wants.

Market signals have not always been clear and consistent with respect to technology development. A prime example is the experience of the pollution control industry in the United States. There is evidence that changing signals given by the federal government—especially indications in the early 1980s that the government would not seriously enforce pollution controls—halted much ongoing research and gave other countries an edge in marketing pollution control technologies.

Regulations. Some environmental laws place more stringent requirements on new products or plants than on existing ones, which discourages the adoption of new technologies. For example, utilities have made major efforts to prolong the life of existing power plants in order to avoid the more stringent air quality standards for new plants.

Risk Aversion. Failure to introduce improved technology is often the result of risk aversion on the part of individuals who influence technological adoption in a particular area. For example, government officials who decide what cleanup technology to use on hazardous waste sites have little to gain and much to lose from trying a novel technology. There are few demonstrated technologies, and the government's selection of a novel or innovative cleanup technology would invite legal challenges. Similarly, consulting engineering firms, which tend to play a key role in deciding on the environmental technologies employed by local governments and private companies, may risk endangering their reputations by suggesting the use of a new technology but have little to lose by recommending the same technology used by everyone else (and, in particular, a technology already embraced by regulatory agencies).

Encouraging the Development and Deployment of New Technologies

Breaking through the barriers to developing and using new technologies requires government leadership, private-sector ingenuity, and public support. This will necessitate new pricing mechanisms, investment incentives, regulatory changes, and collaborative undertakings.

Individuals as well as industry should be the focus of incentives to encourage environmentally improved technologies. Homeowners should be induced to renovate houses to make them environmentally sound. Automobile purchasers should be induced to consider more fuel-efficient vehicles. There is virtually no area of the economy that could not be motivated to renovate, update, or replace environmentally harmful technologies.

Inventory turnover, which is necessary to make room for the better technologies, may conflict with other environmental goals, such as decreasing solid waste. However, the environmental benefits of new technologies in most cases will outweigh such costs, and these technologies should be adopted rapidly whenever there are overall gains to be had.

Design for the environment must take its place alongside cost, safety, and health as a guiding criterion for technology development. It is imperative that the government provide incentives for the development and adoption of environmentally benign technologies.

The role of the government in technology development and adoption will be crucial. General technology policies are now being established by the federal government, and legislative proposals for new federal roles in support of civil technologies abound. There is an opportunity to implement policies to stimulate investment in new technologies and to encourage phasing out outmoded capital equipment, replacing it with new, environmentally beneficial technologies. We favor a variety of measures, such as

New federal tax and other policies, such as enactment of a carefully crafted investment tax credit or "green" research and development tax incentives, to stimulate

savings and investment in environmentally advantageous technologies.

The government must also provide clearer criteria and specific incentives to move technologies out of the "innovative" category. One way of doing this is by fostering technology demonstrations—with the government itself paying for demonstration projects or encouraging the private sector to do so. A good example is the decision by the Superfund Office of the U.S. Environmental Protection Agency to establish a separate unit to encourage new technologies for cleaning up abandoned hazardous waste sites. Moreover,

In the discharge of their responsibilities, especially in procurement decisions, government agencies must make deliberate efforts to encourage new technologies.

Nonetheless, industry, not the government, will be the primary developer of new technologies in response to signals given by prices. Typically, several technologies are available to perform any particular function, and the least expensive one is most likely to be chosen. The existence of a potentially lucrative market for new technologies—for example, for CFC substitutes—will attract researchers and investors. The economic measures recommended in the next chapter also will encourage the development and adoption of new technologies.

As nations confront their environmental and technological needs, major international markets will open up. This should provide an additional impetus for U.S. industry to develop and promote new technologies. Other nations, including Japan, have made considerable commitments to developing and marketing environmentally oriented technologies worldwide.

The United States should promote a business climate to help U.S. environmental technology companies compete in the growing world market and to stimulate the global market for new technologies. It should also launch a coordinated international research effort to develop environmentally sound technologies.

International cooperation would produce faster results at a lower cost to any one country and make the worldwide adoption of new technologies more likely. A separate international effort on technology development could also help less developed countries bypass the heavily polluting technologies that have characterized development over the past century and direct their resources toward using and developing

---

Marketing Environmental Technology

Much praise has been given to Japan for its strategy to become a leader in environmental technology. In 1990, Japan's Ministry of International Trade and Industry (MITI) introduced "The New Earth 21: Action Program for the Twenty-First Century." The main goals of this program are to promote worldwide diffusion and development of environmental and energy technologies through a five-part strategy of globally promoting energy efficiency and conservation, accelerating the introduction of clean energy sources, developing innovative environment-friendly technologies, enhancing sinks for carbon dioxide, and developing future energy technologies.

New Earth 21 spurred the formation of new government-industry-university research institutes in Japan. MITI created the Research Institute of Innovative Technology for the Earth (RITE) to help industry develop environment-friendly technologies. Industry responded enthusiastically and, in the six months after RITE was established, added $45 million to the $80 million in seed money. MITI also created the International Center for Environmental Technology Transfer which over the next 10 years will help 10,000 people from developing countries learn about energy conservation, pollution control technology, and environmental protection regulations.

Despite Japan's highly publicized efforts to take the lead in developing environmental technologies, the United States has devoted substantial resources as well. The Congressional Research Service estimates that the U.S. government spends between $2.5 and $3 billion annually in environmental technology research and development.

The United States, however, has no strategic plan with clear environmental goals or multi-agency coordination to ensure that its R&D expenditures will be effective in securing America's superiority in environmental technology development. Although the United States has had an advantage in developing environmental technologies, it could lose that advantage.

---

environmentally superior technologies. Technology transfer and development assistance will be important tools in this area (see Chapter 6).

Cooperation and collaboration between government and the private sector can also inspire positive technological change. This is particularly true in areas where the benefits of investing in research and development cannot be directly recouped by individual companies. Examples include the Clean Coal Technology Program and the U.S. Advanced Battery Consortium (see box below). In terms of the developmental process, these two programs are useful models. In both, industry and government work together to set the research agenda and to fund and jointly conduct the research, development, and demonstration of the new technologies. Commercialization is left to the pri-

---

Technology Development: Government-Industry Cooperation

New trends in government-industry cooperation characterize recent efforts to develop new environmental technologies. The Clean Coal Technology Program started in 1986 is a good example. It operates through a series of "solicitations." The Department of Energy (DOE) issues a "Program Opportunity Notice," which defines the objectives for each round of solicitations. Industry then submits proposals for demonstration projects meeting the objectives. A DOE panel reviews and selects the proposals to be funded. Not only must the project sponsors agree to provide at least 50 percent of the total cost, but they must also agree to repay the government's contribution if the project is successful. The first four solicitations have resulted in a joint government-industry commitment of $4.6 billion—of which 60 percent is provided by private companies and states.

Another example of cooperation is the United States Advanced Battery Consortium (USABC), initiated early in 1991 as a partnership among Chrysler, Ford, and General Motors to conduct research and development on batteries for electric vehicles. DOE and USABC later signed a 50/50 cost-sharing program, and the Electric Power Research Institute provided financial, technical, and management support for the consortium. The project is expected to cost at least $1 billion and is to operate with a yearly budget of as much as $100 million.

---

vate sector. Furthermore, not only is commercial feasibility built into the process, but the government avoids having to choose unilaterally which technologies will be "winners"—a task at which it has often failed. Therefore,

The federal government should substantially increase funding for research and development, and participate in partnerships with private industry to explore new and innovative technologies that are environmentally sound.

In addition, the United States should direct and analyze its environmental research and development expenditures carefully to ensure their effectiveness.

Legislation and regulation can also have major effects—both positive and negative—on technology development. On the positive side are the so-called "technology-forcing" provisions. These provisions are legally binding future requirements for which the technology does not yet exist or has not yet been widely adopted. Notable examples include the automobile emission standards in the 1970 and 1990 Clean Air Acts, the phaseout of CFCs under the Montreal Protocol to prevent stratospheric ozone depletion, and the ban on polychlorinated biphenyls (PCBs).

Regulatory requirements have also produced innovative solutions to environmental problems. The impetus for the battery consortium, for example, came in large part from California's requirements for a zero-emission automobile. State utility regulations are perhaps the most important factor in determining the use of renewable energy sources (see Chapter 7). And regulatory requirements such as the labeling of major appliances for energy efficiency can increase public understanding and may direct market forces toward more environmentally benign technologies.

Some legal requirements, however, have worked perversely to retard the development and adoption of new technologies. For example, when standards for new plants are made more stringent than those for existing sources, industry may attempt to prolong the lifetime of more polluting old plants. The best solution to this problem is probably to mandate that old plants meet the new standards after a specific period of time. In addition, the basis for many pollution control standards and regulations is "best available technology" (BAT) or a related concept. Regrettably, BAT provisions often tend to "freeze" existing technologies and discourage new technologies. Moreover, if an enforcement approach assumes that only one kind of technology will satisfy the standard, innovative solutions will be discouraged. In our view,

Regulations affecting technology should be based on extensive and unbiased assessments of the technological possibilities and associated costs as well as their effectiveness in promoting technology development and use. Regulatory obstacles to the development and introduction of environmentally superior technology should be removed.

The benefits of these measures notwithstanding, economic signals remain the most important factor driving the development and adoption of environmentally compatible technologies. Thus, it is essential that economic signals reflect environmental values. This is the subject of the next chapter.

CHAPTER THREE

ECONOMICS FOR SUSTAINABLE DEVELOPMENT

**We envision an America in which market prices
and economic indicators reflect the full
environmental and social costs of human activities.**

❖

**Getting the prices right involves eliminating price-distorting subsi-
dies, taxing environmentally harmful activities, and
revising the way economic activity is measured.**

T he economy and the environment can no longer be seen as
separate systems, independent of and even competing with
each other. To the contrary, economic and environmental
policies are symbiotic and must be molded to strengthen and reinforce
each other.

In market economics, prices are the regulators of consumption
and production. They are major determinants of what people buy and
use and of what people produce and sell. To achieve sustainable development, a society must "get the prices right." Prices must reflect not
only the private costs of producing goods and services but also the
social costs of using up resources and damaging the environment.

The United States must deal with its environmental deficit as well
as its budget deficit. We believe that the policies recommended in this
chapter will help do both.

THE NEW ECONOMICS

Economic resources are required to implement environmental protection, and, by the same token, economic advancement requires ade-

21

quate environmental quality. The poorest countries are caught in a vicious cycle in which the environment is degraded to allow economic "progress" (or, often, mere economic survival), and the resulting environmental degradation increasingly impedes economic security.

The sobering examples of some developing nations and of Central and Eastern Europe are sufficient evidence of the need to ensure that environmental and economic concerns go hand in hand. This evidence must also inform basic thinking about economics. Current views of economic growth are overdue for reexamination. Traditional concepts of economic efficiency and rationality must expand to encompass environmental factors.

Economic growth is not an end in itself; it is a measure for a rising standard of living. Economic growth for its own sake was reasonable as long as resources seemed inexhaustible, population was not growing rapidly, and environmental quality was not visibly deteriorating or threatening life and health. In recent years, however, there has been a growing realization that *the goal of economic policy should not be growth per se, but sustainable increases in the standard of living, which in turn must be redefined to include not only goods and services but also the quality of air and water and the natural environment.*

Gross domestic product (GDP) will never be an accurate measure of the quality of life. Countries are mistaken if they think their economic wealth is growing because they are increasing GDP at the expense of their environment or their resource base. Indeed, their national wealth is actually eroding if they fail to make compensating investments in the environment. They are living off nature's capital and being deluded by a faulty measure of progress. Although nations may believe that their economies are improving, they are actually becoming impoverished.

Market systems often do not produce sustainable increases in the standard of living without government intervention because prices established by the market reflect private costs but not social costs. By themselves, market prices do not reflect most damage to the environment. Without intervention, the price of gasoline does not reflect the social cost of smog, the price of paper does not reflect the social cost of water pollution, and the price of electricity does not reflect the social cost of acid rain.

The two basic approaches to intervening in market pricing to control environmental effects are "command-and-control" regulation (for example, issuing permits that specify allowable emissions) and the use of taxes, subsidies, and other market mechanisms that alter prices to promote desired conduct or deter undesirable conduct. These approaches are not as different as they may seem. Both alter market prices, and both are a form of regulation. Also, most market mechanisms involve a mixture of traditional regulation and market incentives; the incentives must be reinforced by regulation if they are to work. However, market mechanisms tend to allow more flexibility and to be economically more efficient than command-and-control regulations.

Increasing attention has focused on using market mechanisms to implement social-cost pricing and to increase the efficiency of regulatory systems. Five types of market mechanisms can promote environmental goals:

1. *creation of markets*—government-issued, tradable privileges to discharge pollutants or use scarce environmental resources;

2. *monetary incentives*—methods of changing market incentives, including direct subsidies, reduction of subsidies that produce adverse environmental effects, and fees and taxes;

3. *deposit/refund systems*—schemes to discourage disposal and encourage central collection of specific products;

4. *information disclosure*—actions to improve existing market operations by providing information to consumers and the general public; and

5. *procurement policies*—the government's use of its own buying power to stimulate the development of markets.

Each of these policies has been tried to some degree, and each holds significant promise. Some are directed at making prices reflect social costs. Others are primarily intended to streamline the implementation of environmental policy by getting more environmental gain for the cost.

Market mechanisms have several interrelated advantages. First, they produce more efficient outcomes. By allowing flexibility for producers and consumers, society can get the same amount of environmental improvement while using fewer resources or spending less. For example, the emissions-trading mechanism for sulfur dioxide in the 1990 Clean Air Act is expected to save society between $8.9 and $12.9 billion over the next 18 years, as compared with the cost of the same amount of control without a trading mechanism. The money is saved because utilities have the flexibility to allocate control requirements among plants, thus allowing control to be accomplished most efficiently.

Second, compliance with market incentives is higher because both individuals and corporations respond more readily to market signals than to rules and regulations. There is a positive impetus to make or save money in an incentives approach that is lacking in regulatory compliance. In addition, consumers do not need lawyers or government officials to tell them that buying comparable goods or services at a lower price is better than purchasing them at a higher one. In contrast, interpreting government environmental laws and regulations has become virtually impossible for anyone who does not make a full-time career of it. In many cases, ascertaining compliance with environmental laws has become nearly impossible both for the potential polluter and for the government.

A third related advantage of market mechanisms is that they greatly reduce the amount of information needed by the government and the public. Their use generally obviates the need to assemble, in one locale or institution, the large amount of information that the government may need to determine optimum behavior. If the incentives are correct, the market does a better job of finding optimum solutions. (Theoretically, an optimum solution requires knowledge of the costs and benefits for each entity covered by the change. In practice, this is not necessary, and economic approaches do involve lower information costs.) The United States has already had some experience with the problems that occur when the government tries to determine the allocation of gasoline—a task that the market performs smoothly and efficiently every day.

A fourth advantage of many market mechanisms is that they encourage pollution sources to control emissions to the lowest levels that are economically advantageous. These levels are frequently lower than those that would result from complying with a regulatory standard because regulations provide no incentive to control more stringently than required. In response to a combination of regulations and

CHOOSING A SUSTAINABLE FUTURE

market incentives, polluters may have an incentive to go beyond what is required.

In light of these advantages over traditional command-and-control regulation, market mechanisms are the most powerful tools for making sustainable development a reality. However, there are some situations in which market incentives are difficult to introduce. For example, pricing incentives for energy conservation are ineffective in rental apartments and office buildings where tenants do not pay directly for electricity, because prices do not have a direct effect on the people whose behavior ought to change. In addition, economic incentives such as liability generally are not effective when applied to public entities, because the government officials who make the relevant decisions are not personally affected by the financial gains or losses of their organization.

Another difficulty with pricing mechanisms is that there is no easy way to determine precisely the environmental cost of any particular product or activity. In practice, social-cost pricing is as much an exercise in practical politics as it is a product of economic science. The politics involved tend to be difficult and hard-fought because the stakes are high and clear to all interested parties.

Whatever approaches are used, be they command-and-control regulations or market mechanisms, consideration must be given to the distribution of the costs and benefits of environmental damage and of environmental policies among different groups in society. Congress and the general public often prefer regulation to market mechanisms because the latter are perceived as inequitable. In actuality, however, most of the inequalities attributed to market mechanisms also apply to regulation. Effluent charges, for example, may be perceived as unfair on the grounds that wealthier companies can pay for them more easily. It is also easier for more profitable companies to comply with regulations.

Over the past decade, the U.S. Environmental Protection Agency (EPA) has gained some practical experience with market mechanisms. A marketable permits scheme for allocating rights to use lead in gasoline proved to be both an efficient and effective way of making the transition to unleaded gasoline. EPA's so-called bubble policy allows manufacturing plants to trade off among emissions of the same air pollutants within the same facility. It is generally credited with saving several companies significant sums of money while achieving the same overall degree of pollution control. Yet another application of market approaches allows emissions trading to take place in some areas subject to fairly restrictive conditions. In several locations, it has allowed some economic development to occur without any further environmental deterioration.

GETTING THE PRICE RIGHT

Social-cost prices can be approximated in a variety of ways—through taxes, surcharges, fees for permits, subsidies, the removal of subsidies, or a combination of these. The choice of which mechanisms to use and under what circumstances is as much a political question as an economic one.

A major direct way of getting prices to reflect environmental consequences is to impose taxes on environmentally harmful activities or substances. Members of Congress and others are increasingly aware that imposing taxes on harmful activities instead of desirable ones would have significant economic and social benefits. *A system that taxed social "bads," such as pollution, would be better for the economy and for society than the current one that penalizes social "goods," such as wages and profits.*

This Commission considered a variety of environmentally oriented taxes and concluded that two were of particular importance and should be enacted. First, we believe that:

The federal tax on gasoline should be increased gradually and predictably over several years—for example, by $0.20/gallon annually for five years.

A higher gasoline tax would be the most effective way of dealing with the steady rise in vehicle miles traveled. The increase in travel erodes attainment and maintenance of ambient air quality standards; exacerbates America's already risky reliance on Mideastern oil; has a major adverse impact on the U.S. trade balance; and contributes to global climate warming. In the past 20 years, vehicle miles traveled have grown 90 percent.

The Commission is quite aware of the political unpopularity of a gas tax increase. Nevertheless, a significant and gradual increase in the gasoline tax would be the most effective way to improve average fuel efficiency and reduce the adverse environmental effects of gasoline. Raising the Corporate Average Fuel Economy (CAFE) standards is another avenue that might be used in tandem with a gasoline tax; in our view, however, the effectiveness of CAFE has been hampered by the complexity of the rules, their application only to new cars, and various loopholes and exceptions. The diverse daily individual decisions about when, where, and how to get from one place to another make gasoline use an ideal candidate for a market strategy.

The figures in Chapter 7 provide vivid evidence that gasoline is used more sparingly in countries that tax it heavily. The sharp oil price increases in the 1970s caused gasoline prices to double at the pump and limited gasoline availability, which reduced consumption considerably. These shocks are evidence of the environmentally positive power of a gasoline tax in the range of $1 per gallon. Providing a significantly greater adjustment time through a gradual and predictable phase-in, and keeping the tax revenues in the United States rather than letting them go to oil-exporting countries, would eliminate or mitigate many of the negative economic effects that were experienced as a result of the oil price shocks.

The Commission is in agreement that gasoline taxes should be increased enough so that the price of gasoline reflects the environmental costs of its use. Yet the exact level of a gasoline tax increase necessary to reflect the social costs of gasoline use cannot be determined based on existing analyses. Many studies on the effects of a gasoline tax have been performed, but none has analyzed specifically a $1/gallon increase. A U.S. Department of Energy (DOE) study of the effects of a $0.50/gallon tax phased in over five years is the most analogous. DOE found that this tax would reduce gasoline consumption by 50,000 barrels per day after the first year and by 550,000 barrels per day after 10 years.

A gasoline tax in the range of $1/gallon, as we recommend, would not simply reduce gasoline consumption but would also change behavior. People would use alternative modes of transportation or purchase more fuel-efficient or alternative-fuel-powered cars. Although the environmental effects of such behavioral changes would be positive, there is no way to know exactly what the economic impacts would be or exactly how much a given tax increase would affect driving habits, car purchases, employment, and so forth. Thus, the recommendation of a $1/gallon tax phased in over five years is suggestive of the magnitude of the increase that would be desirable, but more analysis is needed to estimate the economic, social, and environmental effects of such a tax.

To put the issue in perspective, a $1/gallon tax increase would bring the average price of gasoline in real terms up to about what Americans were paying for premium gas in 1981. The tax would raise gasoline prices in the United States to about half or two-thirds of what Europeans currently pay. Although driving needs in the United States are different from those abroad—with much greater distances to cover, larger suburban communities, and generally inadequate mass transportation alternatives—the comparison with foreign gasoline taxes is illustrative. Moreover, any regressive effects of a gasoline tax could be addressed through various means, as we observe below.

Despite the political difficulties and shortage of relevant data, a tax increase on the scale we recommend would markedly reduce vehicle miles traveled and raise gasoline efficiency in the United States to the dramatic benefit of the environment and human welfare.

The second measure we recommend is a carbon tax, which we believe is the most efficient way to begin to address global warming. The tax would be based on the carbon content of fuel and would be levied at the point at which the fuel enters the economy (i.e., at the well or dockside for oil, at the mine mouth for coal or at the wellhead for natural gas). This would create a broad, effective incentive to reduce the use of fossil fuels, and it would allow the reduction to be achieved at the least cost to society. A carbon tax also would provide an incentive for the development and use of more efficient energy technologies and for technologies that rely on noncarbon fuels.

The United States should enact a carbon tax phased in over several years—for example, starting at $6/ton of carbon and increasing over five years to $30/ton.

A tax of the level we recommend is relatively modest. Because of the innovative nature of a carbon tax, we believe it would be sensible to initiate the tax at a relatively low level and obtain experience with its effects. A carbon tax at this level should, however, be sufficient over a 10-year period to stabilize carbon dioxide emissions at current levels. In the fifth year, it would generate about $36 billion in revenue.

It is not likely that a carbon tax at this level would place U.S. products at a competitive disadvantage in international trade. Nevertheless, to guard against such a possibility, it would be desirable for other industrial nations to institute a similar tax. The European Community is considering a carbon/energy tax, the imposition of which would be contingent on similar measures being taken by other developed countries. In any event, international consultation should be integral to any consideration of a carbon tax by the United States.

One question that arises with regard to a carbon tax is whether actions could be taken by those subject to the tax to reduce or offset the tax. For example, could a coal company obtain a tax reduction for planting trees (which would absorb carbon) in Central America? Such offsets could pose difficult issues of both fairness and feasibility but are worthy of consideration.

Another important issue relating to both a gasoline and a carbon tax involves use of revenues. The tax revenues could be used for a variety of purposes, such as stimulating technological change and investment, reducing the deficit, and offsetting the adverse effects of the tax on low income groups. The Commission believes that the difficult tradeoffs regarding use of the tax revenues should be decided in open debate by the political process.

In addition to taxing social "bads," such as fossil fuel use, a major step toward getting the prices right is to eliminate various government subsidies that are no longer justifiable. This is particularly true in light of the U.S. budget deficit and the recognition that most subsidies work against social-cost pricing (i.e., they make prices less reflective of social costs). Chapter 8 contains recommendations for eliminating several price-distorting subsidies related to public lands and resources. In addition, we believe that:

Water subsidies to growers should be reduced or eliminated.

Water subsidies encourage agricultural development in unsuitable places, deprive fish and wildlife of in-stream flows that may be necessary for their survival, and result in wasted energy for irrigation pumping. Eliminating all water subsidies, however, might result in a much greater demand on groundwater (the subsidies apply only to surface water), and state groundwater withdrawal regulations may not be strong enough to prevent major groundwater depletion. At the least, then, water subsidies should be eliminated when the grower already receives a crop subsidy and thus is receiving a double subsidy. Nearly 45 percent of farmers who irrigate with federally subsidized water also receive federal crop subsidies. Some Western states are exploring how to create markets for water rights to allocate water in ways that would be most efficient and potentially most environmentally beneficial. This should be encouraged.

MEASUREMENT OF ECONOMIC ACTIVITY

Economic analysis has made enough progress in quantifying environmental values that many of these values can be incorporated into the macroeconomic measures used by government policymakers. Even as modifying prices to reflect social costs will give consumers more accurate signals on how to align their actions with society's interests, so, too, modifying macroeconomic measures (such as GDP) will give policymakers themselves more accurate signals on how to achieve sustainable increases in the standard of living.

Macroeconomic measures are standard gauges used to measure a nation's economic health and wealth. However, most economists do not regard GDP per se as a useful indicator of economic progress. They consider the net national product, or national income, a more useful gauge because it at least allows for depreciation of private capital. Economists also agree that national income has to be measured on a per capita basis if it is to be a measure of economic well-being. *Furthermore, to the extent that national income indicators are intended to measure a nation's standard of living, they must include the quality of the environment because it is an intrinsic, necessary component of the standard of living.* Nonetheless, as currently defined, national income indicators do not include any measures of changes in natural resource stocks or in environmental quality.

Incorporating environmental factors into national income measures is difficult. Clean air and water lack market prices; approximations must be made. Some resource factors are easier to evaluate than purely environmental "goods" such as clean air. For example, timber is bought and sold in the market; thus, incorporating changes in the stock of timber in the national income should be feasible. Using market values for timber will not capture the full value of the stock of old-growth forests in the Northwest, but it certainly would come closer than not valuing changes in the timber supply at all.

Accelerating efforts to incorporate environmental factors into macroeconomic income measures is important because it is also a major

Incorporating Natural Resources Into National Accounts: Indonesia and Costa Rica

The United Nations system of national accounts (SNA), developed in the 1940s, views natural resources as inexhaustible. Instead of treating forests, fisheries, mineral deposits, and petroleum reserves as capital stocks, the SNA treats them as gifts of nature with no marginal value. Consequently, natural resources are not depreciated like other capital stocks as they are consumed over time. Because national accounts are designed to measure a country's macroeconomic performance, this and other omissions limit their ability to portray accurately a nation's change in wealth.

Researchers from World Resources Institute (WRI) have attempted to incorporate estimates of changes in natural resource stocks into measures of gross domestic product (GDP) for Costa Rica and Indonesia. By the SNA definition, Indonesia's GDP increased at an average annual rate of 7.1 percent from 1971 to 1984. However, Indonesia is a resource-based economy, and much of its growth is attributable to the sale of its natural resources. When estimates of the net natural resource depreciation resulting from the oil extraction, deforestation, and erosion are subtracted from the GDP to determine the "net" domestic product, Indonesia's estimated growth drops to 4 percent annually.

A study of Costa Rica shows similar results. Using estimates of forest cover, soil erosion, and fishery productivity, WRI researchers determined that Costa Rica's natural resource stocks have been rapidly consumed. The researchers estimated that from 1970 to 1989, the value of the nation's forests, soils, and fisheries depreciated by more than 184 billion colones (US$4.1 billion). This represents a 25 to 30 percent reduction in potential economic growth. Because the SNA in Costa Rica records clear-cutting timber as an increase in income, not a decrease in wealth, when timber resources became more scarce, farms less productive, and fish harder to catch, the national accounts showed that the economy was growing—until the crash in the 1980s. The crash, originally called a debt crisis, was perhaps more accurately a collapse of natural resource stocks.

step in external integration (i.e., in reconciling economic and environmental policy; see Chapter 5). If major economic measures include the environment, economic policy will be sensitive to changes in environmental quality. Currently, the system of economic indicators assigns no economic value to clean air and water, but perversely includes medical expenses incurred as a result of dirty air as part of the nation's product. Such a mismatch between the way society measures its economy and what people value produces major mistakes in public policy.

The United Nations is the international arbiter of what should be included in GDP measures. Its current position is that environmental measures should be part of the "satellite accounts." With this approach, data are to be collected on environmental factors but not incorporated into the GDP measure itself.

Over the years, researchers in several countries have been investigating how to modify macroeconomic measures to incorporate resource and environmental factors. Among individual nations, Norway probably has gone farthest in including environmental factors in its national economic accounts; however, various other nations also are experimenting with including environmental and resource factors. In the United States, EPA's Planning Office initiated a small pilot project to try to calculate an environmentally inclusive gross national product for the Chesapeake Bay Basin. World Resources Institute is working on the topic, as are the World Bank and the Organization for Economic Cooperation and Development.

Resource and environmental factors should be incorporated into macroeconomic measures.

The departments of Commerce and State also should urge U.N. statistical organizations to encourage the integration of environmental and economic measures.

A "green GDP" and social-cost pricing are closely related. Both are attempts to use the market system to encourage environmental progress, and both seek to integrate environmental and economic policy. To the extent that one effort succeeds, it is likely to encourage the other. The success of both will depend in part on how society values the environment. A key to shaping these values is environmental literacy, discussed in Chapter 4.

CHOOSING A SUSTAINABLE FUTURE

CHAPTER FOUR

ENVIRONMENTAL
LITERACY

**We envision an America with an environmentally literate
citizenry that has the knowledge, skills, and ethical
values to achieve sustainable development.**

❖

**Schools, families, religious institutions, the media, businesses, and
government must cooperate in fostering the development of an
environmentally literate citizenry that respects
environmental values and assumes responsibility for
putting the values into practice.**

Sustainable development depends not only on generating new and
environmentally appropriate technologies, getting prices right,
government leadership, and stabilizing human population growth
but also on the evolution of an environmentally literate citizenry.
Environmentally literate citizens understand the interrelationships of
natural systems and people, respect the integrity of nature, and make
an ethical commitment to sustainable development. U.S. citizens
empowered by environmental literacy also recognize the importance of
the democratic process in advancing sustainability and seek to make
responsible choices about ways of avoiding future environmental crises
and of better integrating policies and practices to achieve sustainable
development.

A public that understands and supports long-term environmental
protection will demand that political leaders set goals that integrate
environmental protection into long-term policies. An environmentally
literate society will encourage businesses to incorporate the environment into their strategic plans and will stimulate a new technological

ethic that prizes sustainability. Similarly, such a society will motivate individuals to bring the concept of environmental protection into their day-to-day activities and to recognize the environmental consequences of behavior and lifestyle. In short, in an environmentally literate society, citizens will take social responsibilities as seriously as individual rights, and they will respect nature and care for the Earth.

VALUES OF SUSTAINABILITY

A society's values shape its members' attitudes and guide their actions. Values are expressed in the customs, institutions, and laws of a society. Thoughtfully developed and articulated, ethical values express what is most worthwhile to a society and what constitutes its common good. They foster a spirit of cooperation and a willingness to make sacrifices for the good of the whole.

Although science is at the heart of understanding natural systems, achieving sustainable development and an improved quality of life ultimately rests on a foundation of ethical values that emerge from an appreciation of the interdependence of humankind and the Earth and a concern to protect the natural systems on which all life depends. These values include a commitment to ensure that future generations will inherit a healthy environment, a concern with making environmental sensitivity a part of all human activities, and a commitment to ensuring a better quality of life for all. The values of sustainability transcend political boundaries.

Although environmental values are influenced by economic values, technology, and public policies, they also draw deeply on other sources. Positive environmental values develop and grow through shared experiences—through education, religion, the arts, the media, and storytelling—as well as through individual experiences such as outdoor recreation, travel, and caring for animals and plants.

Destruction of the natural environment contributes to economic and cultural poverty. Degrading the air, water, and land not only depletes the resource base necessary for economic development but also harms the human spirit. Economic and technological development have tended to obscure the bond between humans and the environment; however, the bond is fundamental: biological, physical, cultural, and aesthetic. As a value, sustainability affirms that bond.

Information is the gateway to environmental literacy. Americans need information that will help prepare and motivate them to make and participate in environmental policy decisions. Citizens should understand that environmental decisions often involve comparing relative risks, and they should support the most effective and efficient strategies to address those risks. This will require that educational institutions systematically integrate instruction in environmental issues and related critical methods of problem solving into school curricula from kindergarten through college. In addition, the media must be informed about environmental issues and be able to report responsibly on them. Families, public figures, environmental groups, religious institutions, governments, and private companies, among others, must exercise leadership in promoting ethical values for sustainability. And government decisionmakers must actively seek citizen involvement by providing people with relevant information and opportunities to be heard.

Education. The whole educational process in America must be strengthened. This must include designing curricula that reflect the principle that environmental values have to be built into economic development in order to sustain U.S. and global interests over the long term. The need for economic strength to support the environment must also be included. Curricula must reach across disciplines, taking a holistic approach to problem solving. (In this regard, the climate change issue is illustrative. It cuts across diverse considerations in a variety of fields, ranging from biology and meteorology to economics and foreign policy.)

The study of the environment embraces the study of history, politics, economics, philosophy, literature, religion, and art as well as the sciences. It gives students an opportunity to draw connections among different disciplines, to link scientific and social considerations, and to solve problems using a variety of mental and physical skills. Teaching students about the environment in an interdisciplinary manner will also encourage the integration of environmental policy into other policy areas (see Chapter 5).

Students can benefit from practical training that focuses on community- and ecosystem-based problems. Particularly in elementary and middle schools, field trips and nature studies improve the understanding of humankind's relationships with natural systems and enhance respect for and appreciation of nature. Teachers must have the resources and opportunities to develop environmentally oriented methods and materials as well as the time and financial support to improve their own knowledge of environmental issues.

There has been some progress in addressing these needs. The American Association for the Advancement of Science's Project 2061 on Science for All Americans emphasizes observational experiences starting in the preschool years. Concentrating on such themes as energy in living things, technology, weather, and relationships between humans and nature, this project is directed at all students, not just at those on science career paths. The goal of the project is to help develop an educational system that improves scientific understanding overall and helps equip Americans to deal with the technological breakthroughs that will occur between now and the year 2061, when Halley's comet is expected to return.

At the national level, the 1991 Environmental Education Act was enacted to fill gaps left after the 1981 repeal of the 1970 Environmental Education Act. The new law establishes environmental education as a national goal and creates an Office of Environmental Education at the U.S. Environmental Protection Agency (EPA) to carry out this mandate. Among other activities, the office provides grants for training and educational programs and for state, local, and nonprofit environmental education efforts; fellowships for teachers; internships for students; a clearinghouse of information on environmental educational materials produced by federal agencies; and environmental education awards. The law also authorizes $65 million over five years to support environmental education and educators.

State and local governments are responsible for developing educational programs and many have demonstrated leadership in designing environmental education curricula.

State Environmental Education Programs

Examples of state efforts to integrate environmental education programs into their curricula include:

California: California's Education Code requires all elementary and secondary schools to instruct students in environmental protection and sustainable use of natural resources. The California Department of Education has developed an integrated model for environmental education that ties together topics such as water resources, energy resources, human communities, air resources, integrated waste management, marine communities and resources, plant communities, and wildlife communities. Each concept is further addressed at four different groupings of grades.

Florida: Florida Resources for Environmental Education (FREE) for Teachers is an on-line clearinghouse for Florida-based environmental education materials, programs, and information. The National Science Foundation has granted Florida $7.9 million over five years to restructure science in K-8, lower-division college, and university programs.

Hawaii: Environmental Education in Hawaii has developed an interdisciplinary program that includes marine, terrestrial and atmospheric, energy, and resource management and conservation education. These topics are integrated into science, social studies, mathematics, language and fine arts, health, and practical and industrial arts classes. Students interact with a variety of environments to develop an awareness of and positive attitudes/values toward the environment.

Wisconsin: Teacher certification candidates for early childhood, elementary, agriculture, science, and social studies education are required to develop a basic competency in environmental studies. Environmental education is taught through an interdisciplinary approach. The environment is emphasized in art, health, science, and social studies curricula with the goal of helping students gain an awareness and knowledge of the environment, its functions, and its current challenges; develop positive environment-related attitudes and values; and gain skills and experiences that will enable students to put such values into practice.

State and local governments should continue to develop and institute interdisciplinary environmental curricula. The federal government should provide resources, including financial support, for the development and implementation of state and local environmental education initiatives.

Most colleges and universities offer some form of environmental studies programs; some have developed quite sophisticated interdisciplinary curricula. Stanford University, for example, offers an Earth systems major in which students take courses in biology, chemistry, geology, economics, calculus, physics, and statistics in addition to the core Earth systems curriculum. At Tufts University, the Environmental Literacy Institute teaches faculty from a wide range of disciplines how to incorporate environmental issues and perspectives into their work. *Colleges and universities should offer students an array of environmental courses from a variety of academic disciplines, an interdisciplinary environmental major, and conferences and lecture series that address environmental issues. In graduate and professional schools, there is also a need to integrate environmental topics.*

Many nonschool programs offer dynamic avenues for instilling environmental values. Youth groups such as 4-H Clubs and the Boy Scouts and Girl Scouts integrate environmental awareness into their activities. Many environmental and wildlife organizations offer a rich array of educational opportunities. Communities across the country offer opportunities to participate in recycling projects, nature presentations and walks, and energy conservation programs. An increasing number of zoos, natural history and science museums, and children's magazines and book clubs are committed to environmental education.

The Media. We cannot overemphasize the power of television and other communications media to inform people about the environment and encourage environmentally positive behavior. National newspapers report on environmental events virtually every day, as do TV news and other programs. Television has a unique capacity to reach households around the globe, and it can thereby promote the interconnectedness of people of all nations. *Because responsible and effective media coverage of environmental issues must be scientifically informed and clear to nonscientists, it is important that some reporters specialize in environmental subjects and that training be offered when necessary to meet this need.*

The Arts. The arts deeply influence the way people perceive and appreciate the world around them. They shape attitudes and form values. Writers, poets, filmmakers, musicians, painters, sculptors, actors, and dancers can and do contribute significantly to awakening the public to the importance of environmental values and sustainable development.

LEADERSHIP

American leaders have a crucial part to play in demonstrating how to integrate environmental values into policies and practices on a long-term basis. Leadership guides people beyond their immediate perception of self-interest and helps them overcome their fears of acting in isolation and of having others benefit unfairly from their own sacrifice. While we are not so naive as to believe that short-term concerns will not dominate much political dialogue, we nonetheless share the belief that: *America's leaders—political, environmental, religious, cultural, and industrial—have an obligation to focus public debate on environmental issues because these issues fundamentally affect the quality of life not only of this generation but of those to come.*

Environmental Citizen Groups. Significant contributions to environmental protection in the United States have been made by environmental citizen groups. Environmental groups fulfill an important role in environmental protection as watchdogs, innovators, advocates, citizen organizers, and public educators. Environmental groups have expanded environmental concern and activism in America. Particularly at the grassroots level, they have worked to emphasize links between the environment and public health (among other things) and to involve a broad cross-section of society in environmental issues. They are a critical force for sustainable development.

A number of environmental groups are beginning to work cooperatively with business and industry to identify actions that can serve both economic and environmental interests. This is an example of how former antagonists can be unified by the mutual rewards that sustainable development can offer.

Private Enterprise. Many companies are embracing an ethic of sustainability. This is critical because in our view the business community is the sector that can most efficiently provide the organization, technology, and financial resources needed to design and implement changes of the scale required to achieve sustainable development. Companies that are trying to be leaders on the path to a sustainable future deserve encouragement and support, just as laggards must be prodded along.

Many businesses are voluntarily developing programs to reduce pollutants beyond statutory requirements and to better manage and conserve natural resources. In addition, many participate in government-sponsored voluntary programs such as EPA's Green Lights program to decrease energy consumption (see Chapter 7) and in EPA's 33/50 program to cut priority toxic chemical discharges 50 percent by 1995.

Corporate leaders should make long-term environmental management a basic component of their strategic decisionmaking and planning.

Evaluating managers for compliance with environmental requirements and introduction of environmental initiatives will provide a powerful incentive for managers to work toward sustainability.

Religious Institutions. The growing concern of Americans with the future of the environment is reflected in the diversity of groups that now are embracing and promoting environmental values and activism. The religious community, for example, has become an important avenue for disseminating information and developing environmental literacy. The environment and human behavior are frequent topics of sermons, and congregations are often encouraged to participate in environmentally oriented community activities. The theme of the May 1990 North American Conference on Religion and Ecology, "Caring for Creation," held in Washington, D.C., demonstrated the religious community's commitment to the environment.

In May 1992, the Joint Appeal by Religion and Science for the Environment held a two-day meeting on Capitol Hill to urge Congress and the White House to take strong steps to protect the environment. The Joint Appeal's "Mission to Washington" included prominent religious leaders from the Jewish, Protestant, Roman Catholic, and Native American traditions, representing 330,000 American religious congregations, along with leading astronomers, biologists, physicists, ecologists, climatologists, chemists, botanists, and economists. The group presented its findings and concerns regarding the environment to Congress and issued a declaration that "our nation has an inescapable moral duty to lead the way to genuinely effective solutions." The declaration further stated:

Choosing a Sustainable Future

Business Initiatives for the Environment

The following are four examples of how some business groups are demonstrating leadership in promoting environmental quality and environmental ethics:

The Business Charter for Sustainable Development of the International Chamber of Commerce contains 16 principles, ranging from recognizing environmental management as among the "highest corporate priorities" to contributing to public policy and "programs and educational initiatives that will enhance environmental awareness and protection."

The Global Environmental Management Initiative (GEMI), with 20 member companies, is creating an infrastructure to improve corporate environmental management practices and performance on a continuous basis worldwide. One of its aims is to include environmental concerns in the concept of total quality management so that the environment becomes an integral part of corporate thinking and operations. Another is to improve industry communications with individuals and organizations concerned about the environment.

Responsible Care, a program that is an obligation of membership in the U.S. Chemical Manufacturers Association, requires a commitment to "continuous improvement by the chemical industry in health, safety, and environmental quality" and sets out specific requirements for meeting that commitment.

The *Business Council for Sustainable Development* has declared its commitment to achieving sustainable development in *Changing Course: A Global Business Perspective on Development and the Environment.* The report provides a blueprint for actions by the international business community to achieve sustainable development.

Insofar as our peril arises from a neglect of moral values, human pride, arrogance, inattention, greed, improvidence, and a penchant for the short-term over the long, religion has an essential role to play. Insofar as our peril arises from our ignorance of the intricate interconnectedness of nature, science has an essential role to play.

This historic gathering of scientists and religious leaders also affirmed "the indivisibility of social justice and the preservation of the environment." The spirit of cooperation for the sake of environmental action demonstrated by the Joint Appeal (whose members have deep differences on many other issues) is a model for other such initiatives.

PUBLIC PARTICIPATION AND CIVIC RESPONSIBILITY

America's democratic form of government not only guarantees rights and privileges but also confers responsibilities. Americans can no longer afford to be apathetic about the effectiveness of government and the ability of citizens to make a difference (see Chapter 5). *Americans must insist on and exercise the right to participate effectively in decision-making. This is particularly important in environmental issues because of their broad and lasting impacts.*

Community right-to-know provisions have been enacted in federal and state law and are an invaluable source of information. These provisions offer the public access to information about what chemicals are being emitted from what sources. Such information has empowered citizens to participate meaningfully in industry and government activities to address specific environmental problems.

Industry has benefited from being required to produce information on processes and pollutant emissions as well. Compliance with the Toxic Release Inventory (TRI) requirements of the 1986 Superfund amendments, for example, has forced companies to develop more information about their processes. This necessity in turn can and does help companies identify problems and develop better, more systematic solutions (see Chapter 8).

Like the TRI, environmental audits provide information about processes, pollutant emissions, and compliance status that might not be revealed through monitoring for compliance with particular legal requirements. Because of the company-specific detail they provide, audits can promote pollution prevention by integrating environmental concerns early on in the long-term strategic planning process. They can also lead to early identification of problem areas, thereby providing flexibility for more effective and efficient solutions.

There are certain difficulties associated with environmental audits. Not only can audits be expensive and time consuming, but heated debate has arisen about whether audits should be publicly available. The complex and important issues at stake include self-incrimination and intellectual property rights. In our view, the benefits to companies of auditing are potentially so great that we would distinguish between a complete environmental audit (which would be the company's property) and public reports from a company (which would be based on information revealed through the audit). Accordingly,

Businesses should undertake regular environmental audits and make periodic reports to the public on their environmental performance.

Product labeling is another important source of information for citizens. Standards and criteria gradually are being developed for environmental labeling of consumer products. Consumer groups concerned with labeling have encouraged citizens to marshall their buying power to pressure industry to design and alter products and processes with environmental protection in mind. "Environment-friendly" advertising campaigns attest to the marketability of such products.

Consumer-labeling efforts should continue to involve government, private industry, consumer groups, and environmental organizations in developing labels that are clear and easily understood by the consumer.

A government agency such as the Federal Trade Commission should be prepared to police false or misleading representations of a product's or company's environmental effects.

Investments are another area where individuals can influence environmental decisions by businesses. *Citizens should actively exercise their economic power for the environment through shareholder voting and investment decisions.* This can encourage companies to elevate the cessation of pollution and the manufacture of safer products on their agendas—and can thus promote better integration of environmental issues into strategic plans.

The Coalition for Environmentally Responsible Economics issued 10 "Valdez Principles" in 1989 to help investors make informed investment decisions based on a company's environmental commitment. Other organizations, including the Investor Responsibility Research

Center, provide information and reports to investors on public policy issues, including the environment. Social investment firms and specialized mutual funds also screen companies based on their environmental behavior.

Citizen activism has been the catalyst for considerable environmental progress in the United States. As environmental issues become increasingly complex, the need for involvement in both private and public decisionmaking by environmentally literate citizens will be even more urgent. In the next chapter, we turn to the public sector and the importance of effective governance for sustainable development.

CHAPTER FIVE

GOVERNANCE FOR SUSTAINABLE DEVELOPMENT

**We envision an America where leaders are committed
to long-term environmental protection and to
international leadership and cooperation in addressing
the world's environmental problems.**

❖

**Environmental considerations must become
integral to all government policies.**

T he environment is not just one among many policy areas.
Environmental goals must take their place with economic
goals as fundamental considerations underpinning *all* policies.
If environmental management fails, then transportation, agriculture,
and housing policy also will fail.

This chapter examines a pair of interrelated changes in government that are needed to achieve sustainable development. The first is
to make the environment an integral element of all government policies. The second is to improve the basic underpinnings of governance:
trust, equity, and public participation.

INTEGRATION OF ENVIRONMENT WITH OTHER POLICIES

In the United States, pollution laws and programs are almost
always aimed at the effects and control of waste rather than its prevention. Laws are seldom a positive, driving force for incorporating
environmental considerations into the design and use of technologies

in manufacturing, agriculture, and other sectors. *To become a positive force, U.S. laws and programs must be based on preventing pollution rather than on taking care of it after it has been produced. Until this occurs, sustainable development will not be possible.*

At present, the environment is barely beginning to be incorporated into policies or technologies that lie outside what is traditionally regarded as the environmental sector. There are examples of progress: impact assessment under the National Environmental Policy Act (NEPA) as applied to some types of resource management and development projects; so-called green investment and marketing; steps toward sustainable agriculture; and the cautionary influence of liability for pollution or other forms of environmental damage. Environmental considerations remain, however, an afterthought in most policy decisions. The costs of incorporating environmental and health protection into policies are frequently considered an obstacle to productivity and economic development—if they are considered at all.

Although pollution control laws and programs must change, sustainable development will also require fundamental changes in the goals and institutions of all sectors of society. This awareness is beginning to be embodied in legislation. For example, the Single European Act of 1987 of the European Community states that

> [a]ction by the Community relating to the environment shall be based on the principles that preventive action should be taken, that environmental damage should as a priority be rectified at the source, and that the polluter should pay. Environmental protection requirements shall be a component of the Community's other policies.

The U.S. Pollution Prevention Act of 1990 calls on the U.S. Environmental Protection Agency (EPA) to promote source reduction practices in other federal agencies and to develop and implement a pollution prevention strategy that addresses the full range of environmental problems, including those arising from agriculture, energy, federal facilities, and industrial point sources.

Despite the Pollution Prevention Act and NEPA, efforts to dismantle barriers that impede environmental policy integration in the United States are embryonic. The environment is still a long way from equaling economics as a basic factor that shapes policies for agriculture, transportation, or energy. Indeed, policies in these areas historically have origins, styles, technical contexts, methods, and constituencies that differ from each other and from environmental policy; their goals and objectives sometimes appear to conflict directly with environmental policy.

The goal of U.S. energy policy, for example, is a cheap and abundant supply. Some environmental factors pertaining to energy are unfamiliar, often technical, and likely to require new skills. Some of the adverse environmental effects are expected to occur far in the future (if at all); data on the nature of the effects and the costs and benefits of control are often weak.

A critical mass for change must be developed to move the environment from the periphery to the center of decisionmaking. Doing so will require new organizational entities and responsibilities. At a minimum, each federal agency must have a top-level manager for environmental issues, develop environmental goals, and establish a strategy for reaching them, report on progress, and set up a means for regular interaction with federal and state environmental agencies. The private sector, including manufacturing, agriculture, transportation, and the building trades, must undertake parallel and complementary efforts.

The time has come for leadership to spearhead the effort to incorporate the environmental dimension into all policy areas. Presidential commitment is essential to achieve this goal; at the same time, however, it cannot be subject to the momentary vagaries of political change. Each administration will require the continuity, analysis, and structures that can give enduring substance to the integration process.

Congress and the President should work together to develop a National Environmental Strategy. This strategy should be the basis for federal agencies to incorporate environmental considerations into their plans and policies. It should also be the basis for the federal government's work with the private sector to achieve sustainable development.

The National Environmental Strategy should be a new type of instrument in American government. Existing mechanisms are not adequate to bring about the broad but intense coordinated effort that will link environmental considerations to various sectors of the economy and relate explicitly environmental programs to programs of diverse federal agencies.

The strategy should be based on certain agreed-upon principles, and it should serve as a detailed guide for achieving sustainable development. It should include specific quantitative goals, priorities, and steps that agencies must take to achieve environmental objectives. The strategy should be dynamic and responsive, updated perhaps every two years. The considerable progress that the Netherlands has made in developing a national environmental strategy (see box) provides a useful lesson, although the size and culture of the United States make the development and implementation of such a strategy more difficult.

There are many options both for initiating the strategy and for making the process work once it has started. The initial strategy (or at least the principles underlying it) could be formulated by a commission that would include representatives of Congress, the executive branch, and the public. The commission could also recommend institutional mechanisms for updating and implementing the strategy.

An important question is whether the strategy should include specific budget numbers. Including budget figures to accompany proposed agency actions would improve the strategy's chances of influencing agency behavior. However, it would create difficult problems in terms of meshing with the budget process, and it would also require that the strategy be updated annually or biannually.

The process of formulating the National Environmental Strategy should be embodied in legislation. The legislative mandate to support such a major change in government must be strong and clear. It must state unambiguously the obligation of all agencies to work toward sustainable development. It must establish the oversight and reporting mechanisms that will delineate whether the goals are being accomplished and, if not, what specific obstacles are impeding progress. An office for long-term environmental forecasting, improved monitoring of environmental conditions, a center for environmental statistics, and a national biodiversity strategy (which we recommend in Chapters 8 and 9) would be important features of the strategy.

Because a National Environmental Strategy would have a significant effect on both the public and private sectors, it would require strong support. The Council on Environmental Quality (CEQ) could negotiate the strategy with other federal agencies and the White House (see below), but the strategy itself should be subject to periodic review by Congress so that those who control the purse-strings can give it direction and fresh impetus. Legislation mandating the strategy should provide mechanisms for involving the public and state governments— with states having a direct role in formulating the strategy because they will be responsible for much of its implementation. The strategy should also be the subject of public hearings.

The Netherlands' Environmental Policy Plan

The Netherlands' National Environmental Policy Plan is a coherent strategy to achieve sustainable development within 25 years. The plan defines sustainable development as meeting the needs of the present without compromising the ability of future generations to meet their own needs. Although the Dutch government fell over the issue of financing the plan when it was submitted to Parliament in 1989, the plan has now been adopted with some changes.

Prepared by four government ministries, the plan sets goals for reducing pollution and outlines the actions and financing needed to achieve them. The plan is based on a forecast of trends; both the forecasts and the plan are to be regularly updated.

Under the plan's goals for the year 2000, industry must cut its pollution releases by about 60 percent; growers must reduce pesticide use by 50 percent and consumers their use of solvents by 50 percent; and private-passenger automobile miles are to be reduced by 15 percent. The primary means of achieving these goals are promoting energy efficiency and product quality and reducing emissions throughout the life-cycle of products. Environmental costs for agriculture and industry are expected to double between 1988 and 1994.

Implementation depends explicitly on intensive consultation among governmental agencies and "target groups," which include not only agriculture and industry but also power stations, households, and others. The outcome of the consultation will be plans to reduce (1) releases to air, water, and soil and (2) waste generation and energy consumption. An Environmental Management Act that strengthens and integrates pollution laws is an important component of the plan's implementation.

Unfortunately, Congress is not organized to review, approve, or conduct oversight of a National Environmental Strategy. The fragmented jurisdictions of congressional subcommittees are a major impediment to rational environmental policymaking. More than 100 congressional subcommittees have jurisdiction over some aspect of EPA's activity.

Congress must reform its committee structure to avoid overlap and confusion over environmental issues.

Congress is debating whether to elevate EPA to cabinet status; however, mere elevation misses a vital opportunity to bring environmental leadership to every major area of policy setting. A key role in formulating and overseeing implementation of the National Environmental Strategy should be played by a new Department of the Environment and a strengthened and revitalized Council on Environmental Quality.

Congress and the President should create a Department of the Environment. A principal function of the new department would be the formulation and oversight of the National Environmental Strategy.

The new department would encompass the functions now exercised by EPA. To be truly a Department of the Environment, however, it would have to be much more than a regulatory agency. It would have to take responsibility for expanding environmental research and improving environmental monitoring (discussed later in this report) as well as for such service functions as providing weather information.

Congress should enact an organic statute creating the Department of the Environment. The statute should describe the basic mission of the new agency (EPA has never been given a mission statement by Congress), and that basic mission should be to achieve sustainable development. The statute should delineate the boundaries of the new department's responsibilities but also make clear that this department is responsible for integrating the environment into other policy areas. The statute should describe the way this would be accomplished and, in particular, delineate requirements for the content of and approval process for the National Environmental Strategy.

CHOOSING A SUSTAINABLE FUTURE

All of this requires that the new Department of the Environment have an organizational structure equipped to deal with the new responsibilities. To address the central task of influencing the policies and programs of other agencies, the new department must have offices devoted to energy, agriculture, transportation, and other major sectors. These would be responsible for formulating the National Environmental Strategy and overseeing its implementation. Other changes (notably the integration of pollution control functions discussed in Chapter 8) would be necessary as well.

There was some disagreement within the Commission regarding the role of science in this new department. There was perceived to be a basic tradeoff between scientific relevance and quality. The Commission generally agreed that the quality of scientific work done in science agencies such as the National Institutes of Health is better than that done in nonscience agencies such as EPA. Nevertheless, the use of science is much greater and more expert in an agency such as EPA, which does some science-related work in-house, than in an agency such as the Consumer Product Safety Commission, which does not have any internal science component.

One partial solution may be to include a major science component in the new Department of the Environment but to insulate it from the nonscience components, just as the National Institutes of Health are insulated from the rest of the Department of Health and Human Services or the National Oceanic and Atmospheric Administration is insulated from the rest of the Department of Commerce. The reputation of the new department should depend as much on the quality of its research as on its regulatory enforcement.

Beyond creation of the Department of the Environment, *integrated environmental policies and a National Environmental Strategy require that environmental concerns have a prominent institutional presence in the Executive Office of the President.* In our view, CEQ could provide such a presence.

The Council on Environmental Quality should be strengthened and revitalized.

CEQ's mandate should be broadened to include a central role in formulating the National Environmental Strategy, while it continues to be responsible for innovating new environmental policies and coordinating selected areas such as monitoring. Institutional strengthening would result from changing CEQ to an office with a single head, giving it adequate financial and staff resources, and perhaps changing its name to the Office of Environmental Quality, which could be headed by the Assistant to the President for Environmental Policy.

CEQ's authorizing legislation, the National Environmental Policy Act (NEPA), also has a potentially important role to play in an integrated effort to achieve sustainable development. The NEPA environmental impact assessment process is now the major means by which government agencies are forced to deal with environmental issues. It has brought staff knowledgeable about environmental issues into government agencies and has modified the direction of major development projects. However, the process needs to go beyond individual projects so that it extensively and effectively influences public programs and policies. *CEQ should recommend ways to expand the use of NEPA.* In some agencies, impact assessment offices could serve as the nucleus for further integration.

We believe that strengthening CEQ and creating the Department of the Environment are vital to the formulation, approval, and implementation of a National Environmental Strategy. Unfortunately, all of the desirable changes in government policies and organization that would result from these recommendations could come to naught without improvement in the level of cooperation and mutual trust. Today's climate of mistrust may prove an insurmountable obstacle to achieving sustainable development.

THE EROSION OF TRUST

For at least the past 20 years, the American public has been losing faith in institutions in general and governmental institutions in particular. The percentage of Americans who said they trusted the government "to do what is right" always or most of the time declined from 76 percent in 1964 to 36 percent in 1974 and to 28 percent in 1990. During the same period, the percentage of Americans who thought that the government "is pretty much run by a few big interests looking out for themselves" went from 31 to 73 to 75 percent and, logically, the percentage of people who thought that the government is "run for the benefit of all the people" fell from 69 to 27 to 25 percent.

This decline of trust erodes almost all aspects of governance.

Enacting laws becomes more difficult because appeals to the public for support are met with cynicism and apathy. Implementing some kinds of policies, such as those regarding power or waste facility siting, becomes almost impossible because the public does not believe what the government says. The quality of elected officials and civil servants declines because of public indifference or skepticism about the caliber of those running the government; public jobs have become low-status positions. In the long run, this pervasive lack of trust threatens democracy itself.

The reasons for the public's loss of trust in government are open to debate. Vietnam, Watergate, cultural change, inflation, congressional scandals, budget deficits, economic problems—there are undoubtedly many factors at work. But one thing is certain:

Regaining trust should be a goal of every government agency and employee and of every political reformer and policymaker.

This will require an unprecedented degree of openness and honesty on the part of government.

The public mistrusts EPA as well as other government agencies. Some people, including some members of Congress, fear that EPA will be or has been "captured" by the business community it regulates. Others see it as unduly influenced by environmental groups; still others worry about the agency's capture by its career bureaucracy. Meanwhile, Congress, attempting to prevent takeover of one kind or another, has given EPA impossibly restrictive and demanding laws to enforce while at the same time depriving it of the budgetary resources necessary for adequate implementation.

A major factor contributing to the public's lack of trust is the perception that the federal government cannot make timely, coherent policy decisions. This perception is largely correct. The decision-making process in Washington has become almost paralyzed. When policies are enacted, basic conflicts tend to be evaded or "fudged" because no group or institution has the actual ability to force a coherent decision.

The Clean Air Act provides a good example of the process at work. After 13 years, the act was revised in 1990. The newly revised act contains a number of unresolved issues, however. For example, critical provisions governing emissions requirements for hazardous pollutants are flatly contradictory. One section (Sec. 112(d)(2)) establishes a cost-benefit balancing criterion, whereas the next section (Sec. 112(d)(3)) sets a very specific criterion for best available technology.

Contradictions in policy are by necessity reconciled by the regulatory process, where congressional and public influence is dampened, and by the courts, where the political forces are altogether different. Sometimes contradictions may not be reconciled at all, in which case implementation of a policy may be impossible. All of these alternatives are unsatisfactory from the standpoint of setting national policy in a democratically responsible way.

The federal government's own flouting of environmental laws fuels public mistrust. Pollution from federal facilities is and has been a major environmental problem that raises numerous issues, including liability and sovereign immunity, federal-state relations, the dependence of the federal government on contractors to manage many of its facilities, priority-setting and budgets, and national security. The departments of Energy and Defense are the largest polluters in the United States. Decades of federal inaction and insulation from liability have resulted in tremendous cleanup costs. The exact costs are unknown, but estimates for Defense are between $10 and $17 billion, and for Energy between $70 and $110 billion—and these are probably underestimates.

The traditional but still intact doctrine of sovereign immunity, which shields government entities from lawsuits, contributes to distrust as well as to environmental deterioration. The key to federal facility compliance with federal environmental laws is whether Congress has clearly waived federal sovereign immunity.

Congress should pass legislation clearly waiving federal immunity from the application and enforcement of federal environmental laws.

This waiver of immunity should not encompass the enforcement of state environmental laws against federal facilities. Both equity and environmental protection, however, warrant legal actions to enforce federal law against federal facilities.

Many steps can be taken to deal with the loss of trust and the decision-making paralysis of government. Most relevant for environmental policy is ensuring that government decisions are made openly and with public participation and that the decisions are fair and equitable.

Openness. Environmental policymaking has tended to be more open than policymaking in many other areas, in part because it developed at a time when the importance of public participation was recognized. There is, however, a long way to go before environmental decisions fully incorporate the public's views.

One of the best ways to involve people in decisions is to let them have relevant information. The general availability of emissions data from the Toxics Release Inventory provides an important lesson. If people have the facts, not only will their participation be more informed, but they will also be ingenious in developing ways to use those facts. *Government entities at the state, local, and federal level should develop information so that the public can understand it and find it easily.*

Since President Nixon initiated the "Quality of Life" review process in the early 1970s, there have been a series of institutional review mechanisms in the federal executive branch of government aimed primarily at regulations proposed by EPA. During the past few years, the Competitiveness Council, chaired by the Vice President, has taken on the function of reviewing environmental regulations, but it arrives at its decisions behind closed doors. It does not provide relevant information to the press, the public, or Congress, and it has served as a back-door method for reopening battles that have already been lost to EPA. Although some confidentiality is necessary to allow the executive branch to debate and weigh decisions, the completely closed-door policy of the Competitiveness Council and its use as a secretive appeals court goes far beyond what is necessary or acceptable. This is the kind of activity that fuels public mistrust.

Elsewhere in this report are a number of recommendations that will help open environmental policymaking to the public. The proposed Center for Environmental Statistics, for example, would allow citizens to find information more easily and give them a way to gauge the degree of progress (or lack thereof) toward sustainable development.

Fairness and Equity. An underlying principle of sustainable development is its fundamental commitment to intergenerational equity. As we have noted throughout this report, it is imperative that people behave in ways that leave as wide a range of options for the future as possible. Problems of intragenerational equity are also extremely important. In large part, such problems arise because those who are politically and/or economically disadvantaged are frequently environmentally disadvantaged as well. This is true among nations, regions, localities, and neighborhoods within localities.

Issues of fairness and equity are beginning to receive added attention from both the government and environmental groups. For example, in 1990 the first "National People of Color Environmental Leadership Summit" was held in Washington, D.C. Approximately 300 delegates from minority community organizations working on environmental equity issues attended, as well as 200 "participants" and "observers" from federal and state government agencies, academic institutions, and mainstream environmental organizations. The purpose was to initiate a dialogue among these community organizations and make a strong national statement about the seriousness of environmental equity. Also in 1990, EPA created the Environment and Equity Working Group charged with reviewing the agency's policies from an environmental equity perspective.

It is useful to distinguish between two causes of the environmental problems that are disproportionately experienced by the disadvantaged. Some problems are a by-product of poverty. For example, poor children (and poor African American children in particular) suffer disproportionately from lead poisoning; they tend to live in older housing that is more likely to have lead paint on the walls. Some problems, in contrast, are a result of deliberate policy decisions—for example, the decision to locate a hazardous waste dump in a minority neighborhood. The line between the two is not sharp, and the effect on those who suffer may be the same. However, from a policy standpoint, the remedies may be different.

There is limited knowledge about the extent to which the poor and minority groups suffer disproportionately from environmental problems in the United States. A recent EPA report by the Environment and Equity Working Group states:

> There is a general lack of data on health effects by race and income. For instance, although there are clear differences

between ethnic groups for disease and death rates, there is an absence of data to document the environmental contribution to these differences. Furthermore, for diseases that are known to have environmental causes, data are not typically disaggregated by race and socioeconomic group. The notable exception is lead poisoning: A significantly higher percentage of black children compared to white children have unacceptable blood lead levels. . . . While there are large gaps in data on actual health effects, it is possible to document differences in potential exposure to some environmental pollutants by socioeconomic factors and race. Some low-income and racial minority communities appear to have greater than average observed and potential exposure to certain pollutants because of historical patterns affecting where they live and work and what they eat. Exposure to pollutants is not the same as health effects, but this finding is nevertheless a clear cause for concern.

The political powerlessness of minorities and the poor may result in decisions that exacerbate the environmental problems they face. The evidence is mixed. A study by the Commission for Racial Justice of the United Church of Christ examined the location of all U.S. commercial hazardous waste facilities and found that "communities with greater minority percentages of the population are more likely to be the sites of such facilities" and that "race proved to be the most significant among variables tested" in association with the location of such facilities. A study by the U.S. General Accounting Office surveyed the siting of hazardous waste landfills in the southeastern United States and found that three out of four commercial hazardous waste landfills are located in communities where the majority of the population is black. According to a study by Clean Sites, Inc., "a relatively small number of hazardous waste sites are located in rural poor counties. Although 15 percent of all counties are rural and poor, these counties contain only 4 percent of the CERCLA [Superfund] sites, 2 percent of the RCRA [Resource Conservation and Recovery Act] facilities, and 2 percent of the National Priorities List sites located in the 50 states."

Inevitably there will be some net losers from environmental programs. However, making environmental policy more sensitive to those who consistently incur economic or environmental losses is appropriate and essential. At a minimum, as the EPA Working Group recommends,

EPA should give higher priority to environmental equity and revise its data collection, assessment, and citizen participation efforts accordingly.

Focusing on equity requires a broader vision of the environment. Both the inner city and the workplace are inhabited by large numbers of people but are generally neglected as places where the environment needs to be improved. There is, for example, some evidence that workplace standards for toxics are consistently and unjustifiably more lax than similar standards for the general population. There is also some evidence that enforcement is slower and fines lower in minority communities.

The Los Angeles riots once again called the nation's attention to its inner cities. Numerous environmental problems need to be addressed in these localities—problems including lead poisoning, air pollution, and lack of adequate recreational facilities. And one message is crystal clear: poverty and poor environmental quality are interrelated. Economic development is necessary for improvements in urban environmental quality.

Economic development is also necessary for sustainability in developing nations. As global interdependence steadily increases, international considerations need to become an ever more important part of governmental decisions. Nowhere is this more clear than in the effort to achieve sustainable development. The next chapter describes the international agenda for sustainable development and the policy steps that need to be taken.

CHAPTER SIX

AMERICA'S NEW GLOBAL ROLE

We envision a world in which human numbers are stabilized, all people enjoy a decent standard of living through sustainable development, and the global environment is protected for future generations.

❖

The United States has a vital interest in leading efforts to protect the global environment, moderate world population growth, and improve the standard of living in developing nations.

George F. Kennan, a leading thinker on international relations, wrote in 1985 that the world was faced with two unprecedented and supreme dangers: war among the great industrial powers and the effect of modern industrialization and overpopulation on the world's natural environment. Two extraordinary developments have occurred since. The risk of a superpower war has almost vanished along with the Cold War, and, simultaneously, global environmental threats have captured the world's attention and begun to crowd diplomatic agendas.

The U.S. environmental agenda must deal with the heavy responsibilities wrought by global-scale problems—ozone depletion, climate change, loss of biodiversity, and population growth, among others. These problems cannot be solved by the United States alone. They represent a direct threat to U.S. environmental quality and national security. They place at risk the health and economic welfare of the American population as well as U.S. interests in the stability and welfare of the rest of the world. And they threaten national security in a very direct and literal way; indeed, they are more of a threat to national security than any current military threat.

Domestic and international policies have become increasingly intertwined. In environmental policy, almost every issue has both an international and a domestic side. The policy process, however, has not adjusted to this reality. It still tends to treat the international dimensions of environmental issues as if they were one-time aberrations.

The development and use of environmentally superior technology, getting prices right, environmental literacy, and governing for sustainability are key components of a sustainable future for the United States. However, putting our own house in order is not enough. The environmental situation and political and economic opportunities at stake call for major U.S. initiatives to protect the global environment. *The United States must be a world leader on environmental issues and cooperate actively with other countries in forging international conventions and institutional arrangements. U.S. policies relating to developing countries must be changed to help those countries achieve broad-based and sustainable development. The effort to slow global population growth must be strengthened and depoliticized. Finally, the United States must work toward integrating environmental and international trade policies.*

PROTECTING THE GLOBAL ENVIRONMENT

The natural systems that provide the living conditions for humans and other species know no political boundaries. Environmental deterioration has expanded to the point that no nation (not even a large continental one like the United States) can protect its environment without the cooperation of others.

A strong consensus on the priority of global environmental and natural resource problems has developed (given the current state of information and understanding) among both scientists and governments. As was made clear at the 1992 United Nations Conference on Environment and Development—the Earth Summit—in Rio de Janeiro, a new environmental policy agenda has emerged since the early 1970s. Global in scope and international in implication, it includes the following issues that must be addressed:

Loss of crop and grazing land. This loss is due to erosion, the spread of deserts, conversion of land to nonfarm uses, and other factors. An area approximately the size of India and China combined—11 percent of the Earth's vegetated surface—has suffered "moderate to extreme" soil deterioration during the last 45 years.

Destruction of the world's forests. The destruction of the forests is leading to loss of forest-based livelihoods, fuelwood shortages, serious watershed damage, adverse climate impacts, extinction of species, and other problems. Global deforestation today claims an area about the size of the state of Washington each year.

Mass extinction of species and loss of biodiversity. There has been a global loss of wildlife habitat and associated loss of genetic resources. Continued loss of species at current rates could doom up to 15 percent of the Earth's species over the next 25 years.

Climate disruption and large-scale atmospheric pollution. These problems include depletion of the Earth's protective ozone shield, global warming, and acid rain. The threefold global increase in fossil fuel use that has occurred since World War II is at the root of most of these problems.

Mismanagement and shortages of freshwater resources. Seventy percent of the fresh water used is in agriculture, and half of that water never reaches a plant or animal. Waterborne diseases are responsible for about 80 percent of all illness in the world.

Overfishing, habitat destruction, and pollution in the marine environment. Many commercial fish stocks are disappearing because of overfishing; a number of marine species are in danger of extinction; and coral reef habitat throughout the world is being destroyed.

Threats to human health and natural systems from toxic chemicals. World industry generates about 350 million tons of hazardous waste annually. Pesticide sales have jumped about tenfold in recent decades, and the United Nations estimates that roughly 1 million cases of acute pesticide poisoning occur annually worldwide.

Three cross-cutting factors underlie the current large-scale deterioration of the global environment:

1. *over-use of resources and inappropriate technologies, particularly in the industrialized nations,* which has diminished the Earth's capacity to deal with additional pollution;

2. *rapid global population growth,* which adds 1 billion people each decade, mostly in developing nations and mostly in urban areas; and

3. *mass poverty,* which results in pressures on natural resources because billions of poor people in the world often have no choice but to overtax today the resource base that must sustain them tomorrow.

The United States has a vital role to play in providing world leadership to achieve sustainable development. It has this role because it is the dominant world power, because it is by many measures the world's biggest polluter, and because historically it has been a leader in environmental policy. Without a doubt, the United States has been a model for the rest of the world with respect to democracy and free markets; it also has served in many ways as the model for dealing with environmental problems.

But the United States recently has been perceived as fitful and erratic in international environmental leadership. It excelled in negotiations on stratospheric ozone reduction and has led the world on global environmental research, but it has been criticized for its stance on global climate change and on biodiversity. The time has come for the United States to bring greater consistency to its role as a world environmental leader.

The United States should make protecting the global environment a high-priority concern of both domestic and foreign policy.

International leadership is reciprocal. In exercising leadership, the United States also must recognize the importance of international goals and other nations' policies for its own actions. *The United States must begin to incorporate the international level into its environmental policy decisions routinely for at least three reasons:*

First, some problems can be dealt with effectively only on a global basis—for example, climate change, stratospheric ozone depletion, ocean pollution, and threats to migratory wildlife. Other problems, such as transboundary air pollution or management of transnational water basins, require international approaches at a regional level. (For the United States, the clearest examples are border issues with Mexico and acid rain and management of Great Lakes problems with Canada.) As the size of the world economy has grown, environmental challenges have become increasingly international.

Second, some problems can be dealt with more efficiently and effectively on an international basis. Addressing the root cause of the loss of biological resources and protecting world forests and biological diversity will not be accomplished without extensive international cooperation. North-South cooperation across a wide front is essential.

Additional cooperation among industrialized nations is needed as well. For example, the program of the Organization for Economic Cooperation and Development (OECD) to share the responsibility of testing high-production-volume chemicals for hazard is expected to reduce significantly U.S. industry's share of the costs for toxicity testing. U.S. industry estimates that it now performs 90 percent of all chemical testing; the shared program will reduce this to 25 percent. In addition, the OECD program sets priorities for which chemicals to test and develops common guidelines for testing so that a government can use data developed in another country.

Third, because differing environmental standards for products may interfere with trade, there are strong pressures for harmonization. The current variation in standards can cause problems for either U.S. imports or exports. For example, European Community (EC) restrictions on meat from animals treated with growth hormones threatened U.S. exports; U.S. testing requirements disrupted wine imports from the EC. Such standard-setting increasingly is subject to pressures both from affected industries and from groups with particular concerns, such as animal welfare. National and international institutions are still learning how to deal effectively with these issues.

Thus, the United States has a long-term interest in improving environmental quality in all countries, just as other countries have an interest in U.S. environmental quality. Government thinking and procedures must adjust to the inseparability of U.S. actions from those taken by other nations. American participants in international meetings, for example, must be familiar with past relevant events and with U.S. long-term goals for these meetings.

The American role with respect to international environmental issues must be constructive. The United States has been creative and instrumental in a number of international negotiations, such as those to protect the stratospheric ozone layer. However, both in its preparations for the Earth Summit and at the Rio negotiations themselves, the United States played "a low-key defensive game." The U.S. delegation was assembled late and with inadequate resources. The United States decided not to sign the biodiversity treaty, having given it low priority from the start; it resisted and only slowly engaged in the climate treaty. As a result, U.S. interests suffered.

World environmental leadership entails taking action in international arenas and setting a model domestically. Nations respond not only to what other countries say but also to what they actually do. If U.S. institutions and laws become examples of what *not* to do, no rhetoric will convince other nations that America is in the forefront of efforts to achieve sustainable development. Yet if the United States takes concrete action on an international problem, other nations will know that it considers the problem serious.

INTERNATIONAL AGREEMENTS AND INSTITUTIONS

The end of the Cold War and the rise in the number of democracies worldwide offer the opportunity to create a new, global diplomacy. This is particularly important because concerted international action to promote patterns of sustainable development worldwide is necessary to protect the global environment and to address the tragedy of world hunger and poverty. Moreover, these problems will not yield to modest commitments of resources, particularly in the face of a likely doubling of world population and a quintupling of world economic activity in the lifetime of today's children.

Although the gravity of environmental, poverty, and population challenges is increasingly acknowledged by political leaders, only the first steps have been taken to deal with them. As yet, there is no international response on an adequate scale. The Earth Summit was a strong beginning, but it will succeed only if nations build on the foundations laid there.

The elements of an adequate response are beginning to emerge. The first, on which considerable progress has been made, is the development of a family of international conventions or treaties addressing major environmental issues. Some conventions already exist—on the ozone layer, climate change, ocean dumping, world cultural heritage, trade in endangered species, transport of hazardous waste, and biodiversity, among others. The United States has urged an agreement on forests, and several African nations have called for a global convention on desertification. These agreements are beginning to provide the legal basis for a worldwide environmental effort. Linking them in compatible, complementary ways in such areas as requirements, funding, monitoring, and enforcement should be a priority.

Concluding effective international environmental agreements should become a higher priority of the United States. Specifically, the United States should sign the biodiversity treaty and aggressively implement and strengthen the climate convention, reevaluating the convention's terms as the science evolves.

Another major element of an international response, one on which too little progress has been made, is the creation of an institutional entity capable of developing and monitoring international environmental agreements and of promoting international environmental cooperation. Environmental agencies around the world need a vehicle for effective collaboration and joint action—a means to facilitate their work at the international level. Moreover, the proliferation of complex international agreements on the environment and resources will lead to a crazy-quilt of laws and policies unless there is an international environmental entity working to ensure coordination and effective implementation.

The United Nations would be the logical home for this institution, and the U.N. Environment Programme (UNEP) is the logical place to start building it. UNEP has operated as a small catalytic agency and has accomplished a surprising amount with extremely limited resources and an inadequate mandate. It is time for UNEP to evolve to meet the needs of the 1990s and beyond.

Another area for international leadership is ensuring effective follow-up of the Earth Summit. One of the principal accomplishments of the summit was the forging of an agreement among 178 countries on Agenda 21, an impressively detailed set of policy prescriptions and initiatives needed to promote sustainable development at the national and international levels. Among its many recommendations, Agenda 21 calls upon the U.N. General Assembly to establish a Commission on Sustainable Development to promote progress in implementing Agenda 21 and to integrate intergovernmental action on environment and development.

The United States should actively promote the effective implementation of Agenda 21 and support both a strong Commission on Sustainable Development to follow up on the Earth Summit and a new U.N. environmental agency, built out of UNEP, to promote international environmental cooperation and agreement.

COOPERATION FOR SUSTAINABLE DEVELOPMENT ABROAD

The U.S. stake in the future of the developing world and the nations of the former Soviet bloc is already large and will grow in the future. Yet U.S. policies in these areas, particularly relating to the developing countries, is in disarray. U.S. programs are dominated by a shifting collection of immediate political interests, burdened by conflicting objectives, and inadequate in relation to both the needs of these countries and the long-term interests of the United States.

With the end of the Cold War, there is an opportunity to rethink the purposes of U.S. policy and the scale of U.S. assistance. *The chief purposes of U.S. policy should be promoting sustainable development and protecting the global environment, including the environmental security of the United States.* Achieving this goal will require integrating U.S. policies across a wide front: trade relations, technology cooperation, debt management, and special environmental initiatives as well as development assistance. The scale of U.S. assistance should be larger and more focused. Specifically,

The U.S. development assistance program and other U.S. policies affecting developing countries should be reoriented and enhanced to achieve sustainable development and to protect the global environment.

The new U.S. program should offer assistance only when potential recipients demonstrate political will and commitment to performance and should be viewed as a long-term investment that can yield large benefits for this country: more prosperous trading partners, greater prospects for democracy and stability, reduced international tension, a safer global environment, and enhanced international cooperation on U.S. objectives. Those objectives range from halting nuclear weapons proliferation and slowing the buildup of conventional arms to controlling illegal immigration and drug trafficking.

Developing Countries. Most of the poverty and virtually all of the world's population growth are and will continue to be in the 130-plus developing countries of the South. Four-fifths of the world's future consumers and much of its economic expansion will be found there. Most of the world's deforestation now takes place in these countries, as does the worst soil deterioration. Their cities are the most polluted; their children suffer the most from environmentally related diseases. The developing countries face public health and resource management challenges of unprecedented proportions. There is little or no prospect of meeting threats like global climate change, deforestation, and overpopulation without these nations' cooperation.

The interdependence of environmental integrity and economic strength is nowhere truer than in the developing countries. The problems faced by these countries are compounded by the fact that their economies are many times more dependent on the natural resource base than are the economies of industrial countries.

To help address these challenges, U.S. policy toward developing countries should have several related components that are directed at achieving sustainable development. Management of foreign debt is one of the greatest impediments to sustainability in developing countries. A multilateral entity could be established to work with the developing countries to reduce their debt. Global partnerships to stop deforestation should be developed and promoted. At the same time, the United States should continue to exert its influence on multilateral institutions such as the World Bank to promote policy reforms for sustainable development, such as increased support for projects that conserve natural resources and that use resources more efficiently. Capacity-building assistance (e.g., training, technical assistance, scientific support) provided by the U.N. Development Programme and others should also shift toward sustainability. Enhanced market access through trade liberalization will also be important (as discussed later in this chapter).

Financial assistance to developing countries, be it from the United States or from a multilateral institution such as the World Bank, can play a vital role in both economic development and environmental improvement. The overall level of U.S. assistance to developing countries is larger than that of other nations in absolute terms but very low as a proportion of the economy. As a percentage of gross national product (GNP), U.S. assistance now ranks second to last among the 18 OECD donor countries, ahead only of Ireland. (In 1990, the United States spent $11.4 billion, or 0.21 percent of GNP.) Doubling U.S. official development assistance would bring its contribution, as a percentage of GNP, into the same league as that of Canada, France, and Germany. Currently, a large proportion of current U.S. aid goes to two countries, Israel and Egypt.

The United States should sharply increase its overall financial support for development assistance to developing countries.

At the 1972 Stockholm Conference on the Human Environment, the United Nations set a target of 0.7 percent of developed-country GNP for official development assistance. That commitment was reaffirmed at the Earth Summit in Rio. The 1989 report of the Schmidt Commission, *Facing One World,* called for a doubling of development assistance from all OECD countries combined. It urged donor nations to give special consideration to those recipient countries that emphasize poverty reduction programs, spend less than 2 percent of their GNP on military expenditures, take steps toward efficient family-planning policies, or implement policies aimed at environmental preservation. The United States should link its increased assistance to policies such as these.

Carrying out these new objectives will require more than marginal adjustments in U.S. laws and institutions. Stronger and more effective organizational arrangements are needed both to develop new initiatives for international cooperation and to administer an expanded U.S. program of bilateral assistance.

The U.S. Foreign Assistance Act should be rewritten to address the environmental and development challenges

of the post-Cold War era, and the U.S. Agency for International Development should be strengthened and revitalized to give development assistance a fresh start.

Environmentally appropriate technology development is another area that will be critical to advance developing countries toward sustainable development. A key element in the economic growth of developing countries is their ability to acquire and operate new technologies. The most dramatic example of successful technology transfer is the "Green Revolution," which developed and disseminated advanced agricultural technologies to a large part of the developing world. This effort was based on a global network of regional centers, with each center specializing in technologies for a particular crop or ecosystem. A similar network should be established for environmentally sustainable technologies. We also recommend that

An international system of regional centers, including existing national and regional centers and institutions, should be established to develop, disseminate, and encourage the use of environmentally sustainable technologies.

By involving experts from both developed and developing nations, the regional centers would increase the chances not only of developing appropriate technologies but also of having the technologies adopted. The centers would also address the need to improve capacity building and training, especially in the sciences. Financing of the centers should come from both public and private sources in industrialized countries.

Central and Eastern Europe and the Former Soviet Union. The former Communist nations present a unique challenge, both economically and environmentally. The immense environmental and economic problems they face have been well-documented. Their economic situation presents an extraordinary opportunity to improve the environment.

The former Eastern bloc nations are embarking on a massive transfer of economic entities from public to private ownership. *Environmental conditions should be part of each transfer to the private sector.* For example, heavy metals such as lead and mercury are a major problem in these countries, and any manufacturing entity that uses or emits heavy metals and that is proposed for privatization should be required to submit to the relevant government a plan for reducing or eliminating the discharge of these metals into the environment. Similar steps could be taken with respect to agricultural practices. Such measures would allow economic development and environmental improvement to proceed hand in hand.

The United States should urge the former Eastern bloc nations to incorporate environmental considerations into their economic reforms and should provide technical assistance to implement such measures.

CURBING POPULATION GROWTH

Curbing population growth is essential to reducing the economic disparity between developed and developing countries and to achieving sustainable development. World population now exceeds 5.3 billion and is on a path toward doubling by the middle of the next century. The hope that stability will follow this doubling is now seriously in question. Population growth may continue into the middle of the twenty-second century, perhaps exceeding 14 billion before finally stabilizing. The World Bank's "standard projection" indicates that global population will not stabilize at less than 12.4 billion. The speed of population growth is staggering. It was not until 1800 that total global population reached 1 billion; now world population *increases* by a billion people every decade.

Historically, population growth rates have been highest among the wealthier, industrializing countries. In developing countries, high mortality rates checked population growth regardless of high birth rates. After World War II, however, technologies for improved health, hygiene, and sanitation became available in developing countries, quickly lowering mortality rates. Because birth rates remained high, population growth rates soared.

In the next 35 years, 95 percent of global population growth will be in developing countries, and 85 percent of that growth will be in cities, where the rate of increase will exceed 3 percent per year. In developed countries, the average birth rate is 1.9 children per couple, below "replacement value." In the United States, as in most developed countries, future population growth will be due to extended life expectancy, which in the United States is projected to rise from 73 years to almost 79 years by 2025, and to immigration. In 1990, immigration accounted for almost 30 percent of the increase in U.S. population.

The relationship between population growth and environmental degradation is neither linear nor easily predicted. There is also a crucial connection between the lifestyle of a given population and its effects on the environment. The resource consumption that has characterized the economic growth of the developed countries during the past century and the high-consumption lifestyle of the populations in these countries has been a major contributor to the severe environmental damage to date. Development and adoption of environmentally superior technologies, full-cost pricing, and environmental literacy should work to reduce the per capita burden that developed nations, particularly the United States, place on the environment.

Economic and technological developments have brought about population stabilization in some countries, and, contrary to Malthusian projections, food production has outpaced global population growth. Nevertheless, meeting the needs of a population that is double its current size will exacerbate already severe problems. These include water pollution, air pollution, soil degradation, forest loss (and resulting erosion and siltation), depleted fish stocks, and destroyed critical habitats (including coastal wetlands, reefs, and old-growth forests). More people means more energy production and consumption, more automobiles, and more marginal land used for crop production.

Perhaps the most devastating effect of population growth will be the rise in poverty resulting both from environmental strain on the local natural resource base and the increased number of people among whom food and other necessities must be distributed. Currently, the number of people living in abject poverty—those barely able to survive—exceeds 1 billion and is rising. The poor are caught in a vicious downward spiral because their immediate needs cause them to destroy the natural resources that might otherwise provide for economic growth.

As 90 to 100 million people are added to the world each year, the social and political infrastructure in poorer countries will become increasingly stressed. In the cities, ambient environmental quality will degrade and social tension will rise as demand far outstrips support systems and services. Environmental health hazards will increase, and political and social stability will be jeopardized.

We reject the argument that economic growth as measured by standard of living (e.g., per capita income, agricultural production, education enrollment, literacy, and life expectancy) benefits from population growth. This argument rests on evidence that the standard of living grew in most countries from 1960 to 1984, despite the highest rates of population growth. That claim ignores two critical facts. First, the absolute numbers being added to global population are higher now than when the growth rate was highest. This is because of the 35-year lag time for the children born during the periods of high birth rates to bear their own children. Second, the actual number of people who are malnourished, out of school, illiterate, and lacking safe drinking water and sanitation has grown and is projected to continue to rise substantially.

Thus, we see an inverse relation between economic growth and population increase. This is apparent in the contrast between developed and developing countries as well as between the situation in East Asia, where income per capita has grown fastest and population has grown most slowly, and in Africa, where the opposite has occurred. It is simply implausible that the standard of living can keep pace with the needs of an additional 90 to 100 million people per year, 95 percent of whom will be living in cities in developing countries.

Strong economies are crucial to achieving population stabilization and environmental quality. Economic strength will allow developing countries to devote resources to key population stabilization programs, including health services and access to contraceptives and family-planning information. Economic strength will also lead to political stability and will help increase the options of women worldwide.

Access to effective contraception and family-planning services is crucial to moderate global population growth. *Virtually all reproductive-age couples must have access to reliable and affordable contraception by the turn of the century.* Access to family-planning services and information is necessary to increase worldwide contraceptive use among fertile-age couples from about 50 percent now to 75 percent by the year 2000, which will be necessary to keep global population from exceeding 10 billion in the next century. In addition, actions to elevate the status of women, to raise the economic condition of the poor, and to improve education, health care, and other basic needs will be necessary to increase contraceptive use.

The United Nations Population Fund (UNFPA) projects that the annual costs for providing needed family-planning services, research, evaluation, education, communication, and women's programs must increase from current levels of $3 to $4 billion to between $8.4 and $11 billion annually by the year 2000 (i.e., 7 percent more each year) to achieve the U.N. medium population projection of 8.5 billion in 2025. Developing countries currently pay 80 percent of worldwide family-planning expenditures but are expected to be able to meet only about half of their needed expenditures in the year 2000.

The United States has historically been the largest contributor to international family planning. However, in real dollars, U.S. funding for population programs of the U.S. Agency for International Development (USAID) peaked in 1972. This amount declined significantly in real dollars throughout the 1980s. Even the increases in 1990 and 1991 have not brought the funding level to the 1972 high in constant dollars.

To meet its proportionate share of the U.N. goal, the United States should increase its population assistance to at least $650 million in 1993 and to at least $1.2 billion in 2000.

This amount represents a doubling (from approximately $322 million in 1992) of current population assistance. It is designed to meet the current "unmet demand" (of those who want contraceptives but are unable to get them) in the developing world, which is approximately 120 million couples. While this is a substantial increase in funding, modest incremental increases in U.S. support will continue to address the need to meet the 75 percent target. If services and information are not made available, the overall costs can only rise: more people will require more services, and as human numbers grow, the social, environmental, political, and economic consequences will be more severe.

During the 1984 International Conference on Population in Mexico City, U.S. international population assistance policy was burdened by domestic abortion politics; as a result, USAID's population program was dramatically changed. The "Mexico City Policy" enunciated at the conference prohibits U.S. assistance to private family-planning groups abroad if they are engaged in any abortion activities, even if funded entirely from other sources. *Unless U.S. international population policy is decoupled from domestic abortion politics, essential programs and services will not be provided and population stabilization goals will not be met.*

The United States should demonstrate its leadership in meeting the demand for population-related services by increasing its assistance to developing countries for population programs and services and by reversing its "Mexico City Policy."

In particular, the United States should support the following population-related services and programs:

Health and family-planning services. To reach the U.N. medium projection for population growth by 2025, 75 percent of fertile couples worldwide would have to use contraception by 2000. According to the World Health Organization, half a million women die annually from pregnancy and childbirth, 99 percent of them in developing countries; 25 to 40 percent of these deaths could be prevented. Improved health services also will reduce infant mortality. Historically, high birth rates are a response to high infant mortality rates. Integrating family-planning services with primary health care is an effective and efficient way to provide family-planning services.

Access to information. Women, men, and children need clear, readily available information about family planning. Family-planning decisions are not made by women alone. Men and children also must be educated about the importance and methods of family planning. Only by promoting access to family-planning information and services to all members and levels of society will the cultural, political, and educational obstacles to stabilizing population be alleviated.

Development of improved contraceptive technologies. Investment in human reproduction research by pharmaceutical companies has progressively declined over the last decade, leaving the development of new and improved technologies to the World Health Organization and nongovernmental organizations. Successful voluntary family-planning programs depend on readily available, affordable, and effective contraceptive methods. In the United States, the threat of lawsuits has virtually stopped contraceptive research. The United States should support development of improved contraceptive technologies.

Increased family planning and decreased fertility are most likely to occur when the social, economic, and legal status of women improves and when family-planning health services are conveniently available.

The United States should provide leadership in promoting the rights and status of women worldwide.

Women must have the same legal rights (including property and inheritance rights), economic independence, and educational and professional opportunities as men. Assuring women these basic rights will not only help to stabilize population growth but will contribute significantly to economic growth and political stability.

Family-planning decisions cannot be effectively exercised in the absence of other basic human rights—housing, education, health care, food, and employment. Economic development and family planning are thus interdependent. Nevertheless, according to a U.S. General Accounting Office report, the USAID population program no longer links its population strategies with economic development programs. This is a mistake, for as long as families are struggling to meet basic needs, they will not be able to exercise their human rights, including family planning.

INTEGRATING TRADE AND ENVIRONMENT

Although increasing environmental concern and expansion of international trade have been two significant trends of the past 20 years, only recently have these two trends intersected. As recently as 1988, attempts to interest relevant U.S. government officials in the environmental aspects of international trade agreements drew only blank stares. Signaling a change in this situation, in 1991 several major environmental groups threatened to delay the Mexico-U.S. Free Trade Agreement on the grounds that it would have adverse environmental consequences and to delay action on both the North American Free Trade Agreement and the Uruguay Round of the General Agreement on Tariffs and Trade (GATT) until environmental impact statements were prepared.

Trade-environment interactions will be difficult to sort out, and formulating policies to protect both free trade and the environment will be harder still. As Jessica T. Mathews editorialized in *The Washington Post*,

> the connections cut every which way, often conflicting. High environmental standards can expand exports by stimulating innovation or curb them by imposing higher costs. Freer

trade could improve environmental management or encourage short-sighted plunder of natural resources. This is not a case where the need is to generate sufficient political will to take widely agreed-upon actions, but one in which the right answers are not yet clear.

Nevertheless, liberalized trade will be necessary to improve the global economy, which will allow more resources to be devoted to sustainable development.

On its own, free trade will encourage the continuation of unsustainable and inequitable development. Free trade must be accompanied by powerful initiatives to protect the environment and promote social equity.

The United States should support free trade, with safeguards to ensure that all countries move toward high environmental standards.

Obstacles to integrating trade and the environment go beyond the complexity of each area. A large number of agencies and interests are involved; few on one side are accustomed to dealing with the others. The stakes on each side are high, and continuing effort will be needed to formulate policies that link the various interests involved.

Because there are many elements of the trade-environment nexus, distinguishing among them is important. Much of the confusion over the environmental aspects of trade is due to the failure to define the problems. It is necessary to distinguish between imports and exports, between products and manufacturing facilities, and between hazardous and nonhazardous products. Major issues include the following:

Weakening of environmental standards because of fear that new manufacturing facilities will locate or existing facilities will relocate to avoid environmental regulation. In most cases, environmental factors are outweighed by other locational factors, such as labor and transportation costs, taxes, and political stability. However, there have been exceptions, such as some furniture finishers moving from Los Angeles to Mexico because of stringent California regulations on solvents.

Weakening of environmental standards because of fear that more stringent standards would place products at a competitive disadvantage in international markets. As with the location of manufacturing facilities, this concern is probably exaggerated because environmentally related cost differentials usually are overshadowed by other cost differences between importing and exporting nations.

Adverse effects on the environment from facilities in other nations or from imported products. The adverse effects from facilities can be direct—for example, some acid rain travels from Canada to the United States, although more travels in the opposite direction, and pollution from the Maquiladora industry crosses the U.S. border with Mexico. Product imports also can be a problem—for example, fruit from other countries that contains excess pesticide residues. The more important effects of facilities and practices in other nations, however, are effects on global ecosystems, such as those discussed at the beginning of this chapter.

Undermining of national or international environmental laws or agreements. In 1991, a group convened under provisions of the GATT ruled that a U.S. ban on certain tuna imports to protect dolphins was a nontariff trade barrier and therefore illegal under the GATT agreement (see box). Other U.S. laws and international agreements that depend on trade restrictions for enforcement (the Montreal Protocol on protecting the stratospheric ozone layer, for example) might be subject to similar adverse rulings.

Use of the environment to justify interference with free trade. There have been several instances in which nations have blocked imports on environmental grounds, while there has been widespread suspicion that the blockage occurred primarily for economic reasons.

Harm to other nations through export of undesirable products. The United States currently exports wastes of various kinds and at times has also exported products that have been domestically banned for health and environmental reasons. Such exports clearly have the potential to harm the environment of receiving nations.

The Tuna/Dolphin Dispute

In September 1991, a dispute resolution panel established under the General Agreement on Tariffs and Trade stated that a U.S. ban on imports of tuna violated GATT's rules of international trade. The dispute arose when Mexico contested the ban, which was imposed under the U.S. Marine Mammal Protection Act. The act tries to limit incidental killing or serious injury to dolphins and other marine mammals due to commercial fishing operations. The U.S. government had put the ban into effect only after it was compelled to do so by a court order.

The reasoning of the GATT panel was complex, in part because of the inherent complexity of GATT rules. On one hand, it is clear that if any nation can exclude imports from another nation because it does not like the way in which the exporting nation produces the product, world trade could be severely restricted. The GATT rules do allow import limitations to protect health and resources *within* a nation, but the GATT panel pointed out that the dolphins being protected were *outside* the United States. On the other hand, it is not clear that the common natural resources of the world can be protected without trade restrictions. A recent report by the Office of Technology Assessment stated that the reasoning applied to the tuna/dolphin dispute also might invalidate the key trade provisions of the Montreal Protocol that provide the enforcement mechanism for regulating threats to the stratospheric ozone layer.

Decisions by GATT dispute resolution panels are normally referred to the full GATT Council for final decision. As of this writing, Mexico and the United States are attempting to settle the tuna/dolphin case without a formal decision by the council.

The United States, in consultation with interested parties, should formulate and urge adoption of GATT provisions that prevent trade rules from undermining environmental measures and that also prevent spurious environmental measures from being used as trade barriers.

Trade instruments can also be used directly for environmental purposes. For example, the Montreal Protocol on Substances that

CHOOSING A SUSTAINABLE FUTURE

Deplete the Ozone Layer is enforced through the imposition of trade sanctions. Furthermore, one of the major messages of the report of the World Commission on Environment and Development is that poverty is one of the causes and itself a type of environmental degradation. To the extent that freer trade alleviates poverty, as we have discussed, this in itself is a positive environmental step.

Trade-environment conflicts aside, a very large potential export market exists for environmentally related products. Such products range from large-scale pollution control technologies to "environment-friendly" consumer goods. In a future of increasing environmental awareness and larger expenditures to achieve sustainable development, the worldwide market for environmental goods and services could be many billion dollars annually (see Chapter 2). Some nations will make money in this market, while others will fail to take the opportunity and be cut out of it.

There is a close relationship between domestic and international markets in this area. During the Reagan years, domestic expenditures for pollution control declined; meanwhile, the Germans and the Japanese wrested the lead in the international market for pollution-control technology from the United States. Without the core of a strong and reliable domestic market, a country is unlikely to maintain the lead in the international market.

CHAPTER SEVEN

ENERGY AND THE ENVIRONMENT

We envision an America in which energy is abundant, affordable, and nonpolluting.

❖

The most critical technologies for sustainable development are energy technologies. Highest priority should go to energy efficiency.

Energy powered the technologies that moved the United States from an agrarian to an industrialized society and into the information age. The technologies that have raised the U.S. standard of living and made the labor force more productive have also increased energy consumption year after year. In the last 30 years alone, per capita energy use in the United States has grown 30 percent. At the same time, it is important to note that economic output per capita has risen twice as fast as energy use.

Of all the technological areas that need to be put on a sustainable basis, energy is the most critical. The generation and use of energy are responsible for a large portion of almost all forms of pollution. For this reason alone, sustainable development will be impossible without new energy technologies. Moreover, if cheap and nonpolluting energy technologies were in place, a host of new, less-polluting, and economically attractive industrial, agricultural, and transportation technologies could be used.

A phased strategy is necessary to achieve an energy system for sustainable development. The first step in this strategy is greatly increased energy efficiency or conservation.* The second step is the use of existing clean-fuel technologies. The third and final step is the development and use of advanced, clean, cost-effective energy technologies.

Because the United States and most other countries will be using fossil fuels for the foreseeable future, and because the most effective way to reduce the environmental impact of technologies based on fossil fuels is to use less of them, it is essential to focus on energy efficiency. The federal government's relative neglect of energy efficiency and the overwhelming emphasis on energy supply make no sense in light of the broad political consensus behind energy efficiency and the benefits it can provide for the U.S. economy.

SUSTAINABLE ENERGY STRATEGIES

With only 5 percent of the world's population, the United States currently consumes nearly 25 percent of the world's energy resources. Fossil fuels met about 90 percent of U.S. energy demand in 1990. Each day, this nation uses more than 2.5 million tons of coal, 15 million barrels of oil, and 8.5 million equivalent barrels of natural gas. Transportation is virtually 100 percent dependent on fossil fuels. Cars, trucks, buses, trains, and airplanes account for almost a third of the annual energy consumption in the United States. Electricity accounts for another third, with fossil fuels producing about two-thirds of the electricity.

Unfortunately, the benefits of fossil fuel use carry a significant environmental price tag. The adverse environmental and health effects of fossil fuel extraction, transportation, and combustion have been large and diverse. Fossil fuel combustion is responsible for emissions of carbon dioxide and methane—the gases of major concern for global warming. Oil is a major water polluter; each day, thousands of barrels of oil are spilled and leaked into the world's oceans. Coal mines, oil rigs, pipelines, refineries, and power plants affect land use on a large scale. The transportation sector is responsible for two-thirds of urban air pollution in the United States; stationary sources cause the rest. As a consequence, most of the U.S. and indeed the world's urban populations today breathe polluted air.

As severe as the problem is, projected increases in energy use (see Figure 7.1) will compound the environmental consequences of fossil

---

* Although distinctions can be made between "energy efficiency" and "energy conservation," this report uses the terms interchangeably.

fuel consumption in the future. Energy use may more than double in the next few decades, and even the U.S. Department of Energy's conservative base case assumes that U.S. energy consumption in the year 2030 will be 75 percent greater than in 1990. If the projected increase in energy use is based on today's technologies, the result will be further deterioration in air quality, accelerated global climate change, a proliferation of toxic wastes, and more acid rain.

Figure 7.1. Historical and Projected World Energy Consumption, 1970–2030.

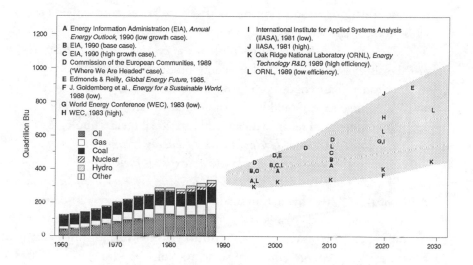

Note: Differences in projections are caused, in part, by varying assumptions concerning energy prices, economic growth, consumer and producer behavior, and rates of technological change, including replacement of capital stock. The shaded area represents an envelope bracketing these differences.
Source: U.S. Department of Energy, *National Energy Strategy: Powerful Ideas for America* (Washington, D.C.: U.S. Government Printing Office, February, 1991).

World energy use projections underscore the global dimension of these environmental concerns. Around the world, 56 million tons of carbon dioxide are emitted daily, and there are 500 million cars, trucks, and buses on the road. The energy needs of developing nations will grow at a much faster rate than those of industrialized societies. Because 95 percent of the world's projected population growth will occur in these nations, economic development is essential to their survival. Yet unless more cost-effective energy alternatives become available, wood, coal, and oil will be the primary fuels used by developing nations, and traditional energy technologies will be the primary technologies for their economic growth.

How, then, can environmental damage be prevented while economic growth is sustained? The solution lies in the origin of the problem. Technology is the key both to enhancing environmental quality and to sustaining economic development. Technology can accomplish this by reducing fossil fuel dependence while increasing energy productivity.

The technological path to sustainable development has three steps. *The first step is to improve overall energy efficiency.* Existing energy-efficient technologies, from lightbulbs to recycling, can dramatically increase a nation's production of goods and services and reduce costs without increasing energy consumption.

The second step is to make the transition to existing clean-fuel technologies. Fossil fuels are not all alike; energy produced from natural gas is much cleaner than energy produced from oil or coal. The transition away from fossil fuels should begin with a shift toward greater use of natural gas and increased reliance on available nonfossil fuel technologies.

The third step is to develop advanced energy technologies that can harness renewable resources cost-effectively, use fossil fuels cleanly and efficiently, and transform energy into products and services with minimal waste. In the 1980s, this nation made considerable progress in demonstrating the technical feasibility of solar, wind, and geothermal energy technologies, introducing new pollution control techniques, and adopting higher energy efficiency standards for everything from automobiles to household appliances. As the United States approaches the twenty-first century, it must find even cleaner and more efficient energy technologies, make them cost-effective, and employ them in every sector of the economy.

Developing nations striving to become cost-competitive in the global marketplace can benefit from the introduction of economical, energy-efficient technologies early in the building of their economic infrastructures. They can rely on clean-fuel technologies (such as natural gas) and on electricity produced from a variety of clean-energy sources as a means of significantly reducing dependence on wood, coal, and oil combustion. They can utilize technologies being developed around the world, such as the combustion technologies developed through the U.S. Clean Coal Program (see Chapter 2). By pursuing clean and efficient energy production and end-use technologies from the outset, developing nations will be well-positioned to leapfrog past the dirty technologies used in the last century in the now developed countries and to move more directly toward advanced and clean technologies.

THE ROLE OF ENERGY-EFFICIENT TECHNOLOGIES

Energy-efficient technologies available today can perform the same tasks, produce the same products, and provide comfort and convenience comparable to traditional technologies while using a fraction of the energy. For example, compact fluorescent lamps are "off-the-shelf" devices so efficient that an 18-watt fluorescent provides as much light as a 75-watt incandescent bulb—yet the fluorescent lamp lasts 10 times longer and uses only one-fourth as much electricity. Expanded use of recycling, another energy-efficient practice, could save enormous quantities of energy. As noted, the United States consumes 25 percent of the world's fossil fuels; it also uses 33 percent of the paper and 24 percent of the aluminum consumed globally each year. The manufacture of paper, glass, and metal products from recycled materials generally uses less energy than would be needed to produce them from raw materials.

Efficiency is the most cost-effective and environmentally beneficial approach for resolving the nation's major energy problems at this time. *Although a totally nonpolluting, nonfossil energy system may be feasible in the future, at present the most needed and desirable technologies are those that increase energy efficiency.*

Estimates vary on how much the United States can improve energy efficiency. The Green Lights program initiated in 1991 by the U.S. Environmental Protection Agency (EPA) illustrates that there is room for improvement in energy consumption that can simultaneously benefit the economy. Green Lights, a voluntary program, encourages corporations to reduce their use of electricity for lighting by adopting energy-efficiency measures that save money. EPA estimates that the program can reduce the total demand for electricity lighting by at least 20 percent and eventually by as much as 60 percent. According to the Electric Power Research Institute, if all of the current most energy-efficient technologies were adopted, the United States would reduce up to 44 percent of its projected energy consumption by the year 2000. And the United States Energy Association, a broad coalition of energy-related organizations, estimates that Americans could reduce their $440 billion annual energy bill by at least $100 billion through energy efficiency. If the price of electricity were to reflect its average lower environmental impacts, the opportunities would be even more compelling.

Political support for energy efficiency is strong. Both industry and environmentalists favor it. When the U.S. Department of Energy (DOE) held an extended series of public hearings throughout the country in the course of developing the National Energy Strategy, it heard a consistently loud and clear message about increasing the emphasis on conservation and efficiency. The economic case for energy efficiency is equally persuasive. Opportunities for residences, factories, farms, and offices to save energy at a profit are innumerable.

The states and the federal government should develop and maintain programs that provide incentives for energy efficiency, such as allowing utilities to earn as much by improving efficiency as by increasing production.

The President and Congress should give highest priority to forging a comprehensive strategy for energy efficiency in the United States. This strategy should contain explicit energy-efficiency goals for each sector of the economy, including dates for meeting these targets, and should be clearly coordinated with the National Environmental Strategy we recommended in Chapter 5. The energy strategy must recognize that energy pricing is a key to energy efficiency. The states should continue to encourage utilities to promote efficiency by applying least-cost planning principles to rates and to utility construction.

What are the obstacles to more efficient use of energy? Why have existing energy-efficient technologies not been widely adopted? Although research is needed to develop the next generation of energy-saving technologies, enough technologies are now available that are both proven and economically competitive that the United States would be foolish not to use them. Unfortunately, as discussed in Chapter 2 with regard to superior technology, individuals and companies often are unaware of energy-efficient technologies or do not realize that using them saves money. Moreover, sometimes the market itself obscures potential savings. Most home buyers, for example, focus on the selling price of a house and purchase as much house as they can afford, often giving no thought to the possible long-range savings of buying a more energy-efficient house. Thus, there is little incentive for builders to maximize the energy efficiency of new homes.

CHOOSING A SUSTAINABLE FUTURE

Perhaps the main obstacle to increased governmental emphasis on efficiency is the fragmented nature of public support. Because the benefits of efficiency are widespread and there is no energy-efficiency industry per se, efficiency advocates cannot compete with the stronger coal or oil advocates. As a result, efficiency programs are the first to go when budgets are reduced. DOE funding for energy-efficiency research and development has averaged less than 5 percent of all energy research and development. In the past, energy policies have placed more emphasis on energy supply than on energy efficiency. These priorities now must be reversed.

The inadequacy of current efficiency efforts should not obscure the very significant progress made in the past two decades. For example, cars sold in 1990 average more than twice as many miles per gallon as 1972 models. In fact, the United States seems to have undergone a historic transition since the early 1970s: although energy and the economy are inextricably linked, economic growth itself has been decoupled from the increased use of energy and materials. Between 1973 and 1986, U.S. consumption of primary energy and materials remained virtually unchanged while the gross national product increased 35 percent. The same pattern has been true in other developed nations. Nevertheless, future economic growth, particularly in developing countries, will require more energy consumption.

THE TRANSITION TO CLEAN FUEL TECHNOLOGIES

Curbing America's fossil fuel appetite through increased energy efficiency cannot happen overnight. *To ease the transition from today's high energy consumption path to a sustainable path based on renewable resources and other advanced energy technologies, the United States must make effective use of the cleanest fuels available right now. Natural gas is one choice for such a transition; nuclear power may be another.*

Natural Gas. Of all the fossil fuels available today, natural gas is the cleanest. Sulfur dioxide and particulate emissions from natural gas are negligible. In addition, natural gas emits less than two-thirds of the carbon dioxide emitted from oil and slightly more than half the carbon dioxide from coal. Current forecasts regarding natural gas fuel prices and availability indicate that supplies will be abundant and economical for years to come. As advanced energy technologies push power-plant efficiencies from the present 30 percent range to a projected 50 to 60 percent, the use of natural gas as a transition fuel to generate power to supply efficient, new electric end-use technologies makes sense both economically and environmentally.

Nuclear Power. The biggest question mark in the U.S. energy picture over the next few decades is nuclear power. To date, the majority of the American public has shunned it. The choice between fossil fuels and nuclear power is a choice between pollution and the adverse health consequences of fossil fuel-generated power, on one hand, and fear of a nuclear accident and problems with nuclear waste disposal, on the other.

Two technological developments could result in making nuclear power safer. First, within the next decade, a new family of nuclear generators described as "inherently safe" is likely to be developed. Second (and in the longer run), fusion power may become commercially feasible. These developments, combined with concern over the inevitable emissions of air pollutants in urban areas and carbon dioxide from fossil fuel combustion, could make nuclear power a desirable energy option. *Therefore, research should continue on improved models of fission reactors and on nuclear fusion to keep nuclear options open.*

THE DEVELOPMENT OF ADVANCED ENERGY TECHNOLOGIES

Advanced energy technologies comprise those based on renewable resources, end-use technologies, and hydrogen-based technologies.

Renewables. Renewable resources include a wide range of resources and technologies. Some, such as hydro and wind, are among the oldest known to humankind. Others, such as photovoltaics, are on the cutting edge of scientific and technological research.

In the 1980s, the technical feasibility of renewable energy technologies was demonstrated. Today, for example, there are more than 15,000 wind turbines in California producing over 2.5 billion kilowatt-hours of electricity annually—enough electricity to serve half a million homes. Solar thermal systems are widely used for water and space heating throughout the world. More than 1 million homes in the United States have solar-powered heaters. In the Middle East, rooftop solar collectors provide up to 65 percent of the energy needed to heat domestic hot water.

Despite the technological advances of the past decade, the cost of renewables in many applications still remains higher than that of fossil fuel alternatives. Photovoltaic systems, for example, show promise even though they are among the most expensive renewable technology options currently available. Other technologies, however, such as solar heating and wind power, are economically competitive now. *The challenge of the 1990s will be to reduce renewable technology costs and to move to full-cost energy pricing so that renewable energy can compete more cost-effectively with fossil fuels.* The disproportionately small amount of government research and development funding for renewables (see Figure 7.2) is another obstacle to the development and use of renewable sources of energy.

The Department of Energy's research and development budget should be reoriented to emphasize renewable and nonfossil fuel sources of energy.

Other obstacles to the use of more renewable energy sources are as wide-ranging as the sources themselves. Although hydropower, for instance, has been used for a long time, further large-scale hydro development is unlikely because dams already occupy most available sites. Similarly, geothermal energy is constrained by the limited number of suitable geographical sites. Solar-thermal energy technologies often face the same obstacles as efficiency technologies: economically competitive applications do exist but are not widely known or are not adopted because of marketing focuses on initial costs rather than on life-cycle benefits.

While the diversity of renewables makes generalization difficult, on balance they present far fewer adverse environmental effects than do fossil fuels. However, this does not mean that renewable energy sources

Figure 7.2. Approximate U.S. Department of Energy Research and Development Budget Authorizations for Energy Sources, FY1991.

Energy Source	Percentage of Total	Authorized Funds ($M)
Solar renewables	9	130
Conservation	12	173
Nuclear fission	15	219
Magnetic fusion	22	320
Fossil fuels	40	596
Electric and energy storage systems	2	39

Source: American Academy of Science (AAS), *Research and Development FY1991* (Washington, D.C.: AAS, 1990). Adopted from DOE FY1991 budget justification.

are without adverse effects. Hydropower projects require land and disrupt the ecosystems of free-flowing streams. Wind turbines, because of their large land requirements per unit of energy produced, affect plants and animals, including critical habitats for endangered species. In addition, people who live near the wind farms of southern California are concerned about their aesthetic impact. Local opposition to renewable energy projects because of their adverse effects has been a major deterrent in California, as it might be in the rest of the nation. Thus, public policies that value the full range of costs and benefits associated with fossil and nonfossil fuel energy options are needed.

End-Use Technologies. As the technologies that actually use energy can be expected to change, these changes in turn will significantly influence the amount and type of energy that is produced. Many of the most fuel-efficient technologies currently being developed are electric technologies. The most environmentally beneficial future applications of electric technologies are likely to be in the field of transportation. Transportation accounts for nearly one-third of all U.S. fossil fuel consumption today and produces a large percentage of air pollution. Although vehicle fleet fuel efficiency has improved dramatically in recent years, efficiency gains per vehicle-mile are offset by the higher number of vehicles on the road traveling more miles each year (see Figure 7.3).

Clean, energy-efficient electric vehicles and electrified mass transit offer promising solutions to America's growing transportation and urban environmental problems. Electric vehicles can be up to 97 percent cleaner than their gasoline-powered counterparts and up to 88 percent cleaner than vehicles burning methanol, natural gas, or propane. An electric vehicle in California produces less than half as much carbon dioxide as a gasoline-powered vehicle. Electric transportation technologies offer the promise of large-scale, cost-effective, environmentally sustainable commercial applications.

Hydrogen. A number of experts believe that the world will eventually shift to a hydrogen-based economy. Hydrogen is an entirely nonpolluting fuel whose supply is inexhaustible; it can readily be used as either a liquid or a gas. The catch is that hydrogen (like electricity) must be produced by another energy source. Most experts who favor this fuel envision nuclear fusion as the method used to manufacture hydrogen, but clearly a great deal is still unknown about both its feasibility and environmental effects.

Whether or not hydrogen is destined to be the fuel of the future, speculation about it underscores the need to engage in long-range energy technology planning for both economic and environmental reasons. If the United States is to develop technologies to have an edge on the market, it must do so before others do. And, in general, if the United States is to remain competitive over the long run, the technologies it develops must be truly sustainable. This will depend on the federal government investing more resources in research and development of low-polluting, energy-efficient technologies.

MOVING ONTO A SUSTAINABLE ENERGY PATH

How does America get on the right energy path? As with sustainable development itself, the answer lies not only in technology but also in economics, values and information, and governance.

Economics. The price of fossil fuels in the United States does not reflect the environmental costs that society must pay for their use. Consequently, consumption is higher than is in society's best interests. The incentives for greater efficiency are weak, and more environmentally compatible sources of energy are not cost-competitive.

The case of gasoline vividly illustrates the relationship between price and use. Figure 7.3 shows that U.S. gasoline prices, in constant dollars, are relatively low. A gallon of gasoline in 1992 costs about the same as it did in 1971 and less than in 1950. The result, not surprisingly, is that people are driving more and are less concerned with buying fuel-efficient cars than they were a few years ago.

Figure 7.4 shows the steady upward trend in vehicle miles traveled. By comparing different countries, Figure 7.5 shows the direct relationship of gasoline prices and gasoline consumption. Figure 7.6 shows the relationship between gasoline prices and automobile fuel-use efficiency. The conclusion is clear: if the United States wants to reduce petroleum use and increase vehicle efficiency, the most direct and effective way is to ensure that fuel costs reflect the environmental costs of consuming them.

If the prices of coal, oil, and natural gas were to include social costs—for example, the cost of their contributions to the pollution of urban areas and to global climate change—a number of energy-efficient technologies such as renewable energy and electric transportation would become more economically competitive. Not only would society use less of the polluting fuels, but industry would have an incentive to market nonfossil fuels, and consumers to use such fuels.

Figure 7.3. U.S. Gasoline Prices, $1992.

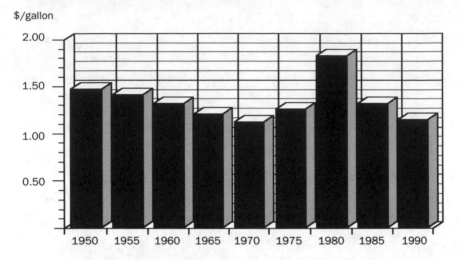

$/gallon

Source: U.S. Department of Energy, Energy Information Administration, *Annual Energy Outlook 1990* (Washington, D.C.:U.S. Department of Energy, 1990).

Figure 7.4. Trends in U.S. Vehicle Miles Traveled (All Vehicles).

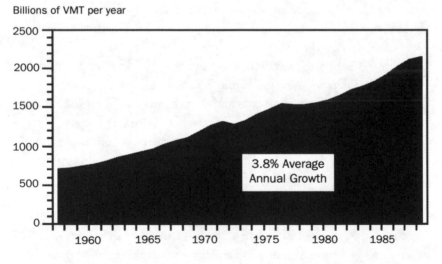

Billions of VMT per year

3.8% Average Annual Growth

Source: James J. MacKenzie, Roger C. Dower, and Donald D.T. Chen, *The Going Rate: What It Really Costs to Drive* (Washington, D.C.: World Resources Institute, June 1992), p. 2.

CHOOSING A SUSTAINABLE FUTURE

Figure 7.5. Gasoline Prices and Per Capita Gasoline Consumption.

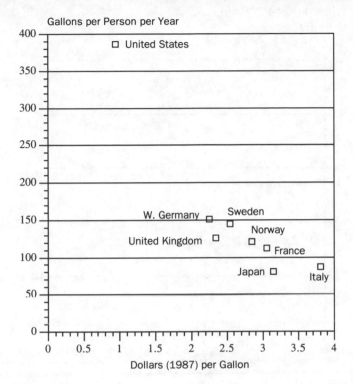

Gallons per Person per Year

□ United States

W. Germany □   Sweden

United Kingdom □   □ Norway
         □ □ France
    Japan □   □
              Italy

Dollars (1987) per Gallon

Source: James J. Mackenzie, *Toward a Sustainable Energy Future: The Critical Role of Rational Energy Pricing* (Washington, D.C.: World Resources Institute, May 1991), p. 7.

Chapter 3 discussed several ways to implement new pricing strategies. Although these measures require more detailed analysis, we believe that

Implementing the gasoline and carbon taxes recommended in Chapter 3 would contribute significantly to putting America on an energy path consistent with sustainable development.

Values and Information. As discussed in Chapter 4, underlying both economic measures and consumer responses are the values that society holds with respect to the environment. Prices are a reflection of those values. If the nation highly values a healthy environment and

Figure 7.6. 1987 Gasoline Prices in U.S. and Europe and Car/Truck Fleet Efficiencies.

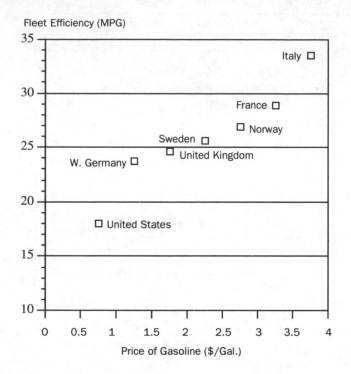

Source: James J. MacKenzie, *Toward a Sustainable Energy Future: The Critical Role of Rational Energy Pricing* (Washington, D.C.: World Resources Institute, May 1991), p. 6.

understands the environmental implications of energy use, it will be more likely to accept higher prices on gasoline and other fossil fuels and to invest more in efficiency and renewables.

If consumers are to respond to prices in a way that promotes sustainable development, they must receive adequate, accurate, and relevant information. If they cannot compare the fuel efficiency of different automobiles, for instance, raising fuel prices will have less impact on their decisions to buy fuel-efficient automobiles. The EPA fuel efficiency stickers on new cars facilitate more accurate market responses by giving car buyers necessary information. Energy efficiency labeling on household appliances serves the same purpose.

Both efficiency and advanced energy technologies require greater investment in research and development, as noted earlier. Much of this R&D will take place in the private sector. For example, many energy-efficiency gains have come through improvements in particular manufacturing processes devised by firms that know their processes better than anyone else and have the most to gain from greater efficiency. In other cases, however, energy improvements may be so long-range or generic that to expect the private sector to finance them would be unrealistic. Because the calculations of individual companies will not fully incorporate society's gains from getting on the right energy path, the federal government may need to support certain types of research.

Governance. Government-funded research, taxes, and subsidies are all exercises in governance. So, too, is direct regulation, which has a major impact on the forms of energy that Americans use.

A good deal of regulation is aimed at the environmental effects of energy use. For example, because of the large amount of pollution that results directly from energy consumption, the Clean Air Act and Clean Water Act have a substantial influence on the amount and type of energy used. Most of the regulation makes fossil fuels more expensive, as when power plants are required to install scrubbers to control sulfur dioxide caused by burning coal. The expense of the scrubbers provides an incentive for power plants to use fuels that emit less sulfur dioxide.

Regulation of utility companies is largely in the hands of state public utility commissions. A recent study for World Resources Institute found that the use of renewable resources to generate electricity within a state was related more to the regulatory policies and practices of the state utility commission than to the actual availability of renewable resources. States that have controlled environmental costs through least-cost planning use renewable fuel sources most. These states also vigorously pursue energy efficiency.

Regulation and price can be intermingled. One of the major forces for energy efficiency today is the effort being made by state public utility regulators across the country to make energy costs reflect environmental costs and to allow utilities to make money by selling efficiency measures, an effort we endorse and encourage.

Regulators should tap the power of the marketplace to provide the economic signals and financial incentives necessary to achieve environmental and social policy objectives. In southern California, the regional South

Coast Air Quality Management District has approved an innovative, free-market approach to pollution control that will eliminate many of the command-and-control regulations for many stationary sources, including both large and small emitters. Under the Regional Clean Air Incentives Market (RECLAIM) program, companies will still have to meet strict air emission limits, but they can do so either by reducing their own emissions or by purchasing "pollution rights" from other companies that have controlled emissions beyond their cleanup targets. In this way, the marketplace will find the least expensive way to achieve required emission reductions, saving local industry hundreds of millions of dollars each year and accelerating the region's progress toward its clean air goals.

This kind of innovative "permit trading" program operates within a framework of preestablished environmental goals. Once the level of emission reductions and the timeframe for these reductions are set, market mechanisms can be used to select the most efficient means of achieving them. Market trading systems offer incentives for innovation and efficiency without many of the political and administrative problems likely to accompany direct taxing systems.

While a new emphasis on energy efficiency, advanced energy technologies, and clean fuels is clearly and urgently needed, our nation faces other compelling questions about how best to curb pollution from existing sources. Government regulation is an integral component to steer the United States toward sustainable development. The next chapter highlights shortcomings of the present pollution control system and identifies ways to improve it.

CHAPTER EIGHT

PREVENTING POLLUTION

**We envision an America in which the entire
life-cycle of a product is part
of a strategy of waste reduction
and pollution prevention.**

❖

**Efforts to halt pollution should become
more integrated and holistic; pollution prevention
should take priority over pollution control.**

Certain manufactured chemicals have thinned the protective stratospheric ozone layer so that the sun's rays can cause increasing cases of skin cancers and eye cataracts. Human activity has added huge amounts of carbon dioxide to the atmosphere, which has led or may lead to the sun's heat increasing at the Earth's surface to produce global warming. Thus, the source of life and energy on Earth—the sun—has also become the symbol of the human power to alter the planet and the urgency of bringing that power under control.

The nature of the pollution problems faced by the United States has changed over the years. Yet U.S. laws, programs, and thinking are still based on a picture of pollution caused by individual industrial plants having local effects on a single part of the environment. There are still situations that fit this description, but they are a shrinking minority. This country's pollution problems are now more likely to result from multiple, diffuse sources with regional or global effects on many elements of the environment.

What has become painfully obvious is that the ad hoc and convoluted structure for dealing with pollution problems in the United

States is not adequate to handle current problems or those likely to arise in the future. Modernizing the laws and institutions for controlling pollution is imperative.

INTEGRATION OF POLLUTION CONTROL FUNCTIONS

The formulation of a National Environmental Strategy (see Chapter 5) may well encourage the U.S. Environmental Protection Agency (EPA) or a new Department of the Environment and state environmental agencies to integrate pollution control programs that are currently fragmented along the lines of the part of the environment affected or the type of pollutant to be controlled. Environmental agencies' initiatives to integrate pollution policies will also encourage other sectors, such as manufacturing and agriculture, to incorporate environmental factors into their planning and actions. As it plays out in environmental laws and the actions of agencies, the current fragmentation of programs along media lines (such as air, groundwater, surface water, and toxic waste) is a major impediment to preventing and controlling pollution.

Why is integration of pollution program functions so important? There are at least five answers to this question.

First, integration would clarify environmental goals and make achieving them more efficient. The current fragmentation and complexity of environmental laws leads to budgetary rigidities, impedes efficient administration, and causes confusion.

Second, pollution prevention could become the principal policy and mechanism for dealing with pollution problems. At present, the evaluation and application of pollution prevention strategies is difficult because data are not available, nor is the extensive coordination that would be required.

Third, the reduction of environmental risk could serve as the basis for budgeting, regulatory, and enforcement priorities. Timetables and budget authorizations in the existing statutes are a major obstacle to using a common risk-based metric.

Fourth, the transfer of pollutants from one part of the environment to another through control choices such as wastewater treatment or through natural processes (as in acid rain) would be considered initially and thus would more likely be avoided.

CHOOSING A SUSTAINABLE FUTURE

Fifth, the use of a systems approach would help identify less expensive solutions. The Electric Power Research Institute, an industry organization, has shown that coal-fired power plants, for example, could cut both capital and maintenance costs significantly by designing for plant performance *and* environmental quality rather than by responding sequentially to new requirements under each new law.

Existing pollution laws and programs evolved during a period of extraordinary creativity and action beginning around 1970—a period that resulted not only in the air, water, and waste laws that have dominated pollution control in practice but also in the beginnings of a more integrated approach. This included the 1970 reorganization plans that established EPA and the National Oceanic and Atmospheric Administration (NOAA), the creation of the President's Council on Environmental Quality (CEQ), and the introduction of the environmental impact assessment process under the National Environmental Policy Act (NEPA), the Endangered Species Act, the Toxic Substances Control Act, and the establishment of the Office of Technology Assessment (OTA) in 1974. Regional institutions, such as the International Joint Commission for the Great Lakes, and the long-term planning and management programs for estuaries also have gained experience in applying integrated approaches.

There is now widespread recognition that preventing pollution is more effective and efficient than seeking to limit it through control mechanisms at the "end-of-the-pipe." While end-of-the-pipe approaches have resulted in considerable progress, they do not appear capable of addressing pressing problems successfully. In many cases, single-media regulatory approaches have merely shifted pollutants from one part of the environment to another.

The preventive approach requires an examination of the full life-cycle of products and practices. Evaluation of a new product must consider the pollution generated by its manufacture as well as its use and disposal. In this context, the notion of "sinks," or final out-of-the-way resting places for pollutants, is and always was misleading. Matter does not disappear; very few parts of the environment (if any) can properly be considered permanent resting places.

Existing air, water, and waste programs have overshadowed the further development of organizational forms and laws that are focused on a source, an ecosystem or habitat, or a pollutant itself. NEPA has played a role in fostering external integration by requiring environmental impact assessments of federal project proposals, particularly in resource management. However, NEPA has not applied to most of EPA's pollution control activities, and it has not been used to assess program and policy proposals. OTA has had limited success evaluating broad technology programs, although its analyses have played a significant role in shifting attention to prevention.

EPA is caught in a structure that is oriented to environmental media or a particular problem, while its research, enforcement, and planning and evaluation staff struggle for broader approaches. The separate laws that guide each program use different standards for action and provide no overall mission for the agency.

EPA is working to integrate agency programs using risk as a common metric. Training programs have introduced the concepts of risk assessment and risk management across the agency. In *Unfinished Business* (1987), EPA managers recommended setting priorities on the basis of risk given existing levels of control. That report found that rankings of programs by comparative risk corresponded neither to public views nor to EPA's budget. In 1990 the EPA Science Advisory Board report entitled *Reducing Risk: Setting Priorities and Strategy for Environmental Protection* reviewed and expanded on the findings in *Unfinished Business*. In other integration efforts, clusters of EPA staff are coordinating regulations addressing a common chemical (lead), source (oil and gas), or receptor (groundwater); strategic planning has been introduced; the enforcement office is experimenting with multi-media approaches; regional approaches are being tried in areas such as the Great Lakes; and the criteria for advancement of managers in the Senior Executive Service now include experience in different types of programs, on agency-wide task forces, and in different locations.

The Toxics Release Inventory (TRI), required under the community-right-to-know provisions of the 1986 Superfund Amendments, has proved to be one of the most effective integrating mechanisms. For the first time, manufacturing facilities must publicly report the amount of certain toxics they are putting into the environment. In only a few years, these reporting requirements have stimulated major voluntary emission reductions and pollution prevention initiatives.

The Toxics Release Inventory provisions should be expanded to cover more types of industries and more

facilities, including federal facilities. The TRI should be combined with facility planning to reduce toxics.

Integration of pollution control functions has also been a goal of other nations' policies. For example, in 1991, the environmental ministers of the Organization for Economic Cooperation and Development (OECD) called on member countries, including the United States, to

> practice integrated pollution prevention and control, taking into account the effects of activities and substances on the environment as a whole and the whole commercial and environmental life-cycles of substances when assessing the risk they pose and when developing and implementing controls to limit their release.

Furthermore, the OECD Council Act recommends that member countries evaluate the extent to which present laws and regulations impede an integrated approach and, as appropriate, amend them or adopt new administrative practices or laws. The act also calls for a review of actions within three years.

A number of states have experimented with integrated approaches and pollution prevention (see box). In fact, the environmental area is an outstanding example of the traditional role of the states as laboratories for new policies and programs. California has pioneered most of the air pollution control regulations on automobiles, New Jersey has paved the way for much of the toxics regulations, and New York and other states have shown new directions for acquiring and managing parkland. Often over the past 25 years, the states have been far more environmentally innovative than the federal government.

Given the benefits of a more integrated approach for identifying and dealing with environmental problems and the increasingly positive experience with multi-media approaches, it is time to move forward and adopt an integrated pollution-control system.

Congress should enact legislation requiring the new Department of the Environment to begin issuing integrated permits covering air, water, and solid waste by 1997. Working with Congress, the department should develop legislation for integrating all pollution-control functions as soon as is practicable.

Integration Models

There is already considerable experience with integrating program functions at both strategic and operational levels. Policy planning for the environment (as opposed to planning for air, water, and waste separately) developed over a decade ago in the Netherlands. Single permits for facilities have been used for two decades in Sweden.

Several states, such as Massachusetts and New Jersey, are experimenting with broader "whole-facility" approaches closely linked to prevention. The Massachusetts Toxics Use Reduction Act requires the development of multi-media inspections and the introduction of toxics use reduction in enforcement.

The Blackstone project, in Massachusetts, which began experimenting with these approaches before the Massachusetts law was enacted, provided useful experience from 26 electroplating facilities. Multi-media inspections were found to be effective at identifying violations in all media. Twenty of the 26 facilities had some violation. Many would probably not have been detected by single-media inspections because, for example, hazardous waste inspectors look at waste storage areas rather than production areas. Opportunities to reduce sources of pollution were identified at 16 of the 26 companies.

An integrated permit would cover all forms of pollution from all sources within a facility. For enforcement purposes it might be necessary for the permit to contain limits on individual pipes, vents, and so on. However, the analysis and negotiations leading up to the permit should be based on what will be emitted from the entire facility and on all forms in which individual pollutants are emitted. Permitting is not truly integrated if separate analyses are done for air, water, and solid waste and then mechanically combined in one permit. The analysis must be designed to prevent sources from reducing pollutant emissions to one medium simply by shifting them to another. At the same time the permit should provide flexibility to reduce emissions in the most cost-effective way. Often this will entail such pollution prevention measures as substituting raw materials or making process changes.

Because most major facilities have permits now, the new system would have to be phased in over time. In most cases, state agencies do the actual permitting, so there also needs to be time to consult with state officials about specific procedures, to train those who do the permitting, and to change state laws and regulations where necessary. Five years should be sufficient. *Ideally, integrated permitting would be part of legislation integrating all pollution control functions, and, in turn, the integrated pollution control legislation would be part of the organic act creating the Department of the Environment recommended in Chapter 5.*

There is a difficult bind with respect to integrated legislation. On one hand, it is not possible to have an integrated approach if pollution control laws are fragmented along media lines, as they now are. On the other hand, an integrated law faces major political obstacles, given the fragmented congressional committee system (see Chapter 5) and the medium-oriented bureaucracies that have been created at federal, state, and local levels.

The technical difficulties of writing an integrated pollution control statute are also significant, but they are manageable. In the late 1980s, The Conservation Foundation (CF) produced two drafts of an integrated statute. The most logical basis for such a statute is functional. The CF version (second draft, September 1988) has 21 titles, including mission of the department, research and training, federal review of new substances, standards, permits, enforcement and liability, and citizen participation. EPA has recently considered a new integrated enforcement act and an integrated act dealing with research and development.

These steps would result in more effective and efficient pollution control. They would impel the federal government toward an up-to-date system of environmental protection and away from the current antiquated maze of existing laws. An integrated permit system, with a single permit for each facility, would give the government more flexibility to impose risk-based restrictions on emissions while providing greater flexibility for industry to meet the restrictions in the most cost-effective way.

An integrated approach could also stimulate much-needed experimentation with more efficient and effective approaches to pollution control. Rather than discouraging innovation, pollution regulation should allow the private sector to exercise more creativity, increasing both the efficiency and effectiveness of environmental controls. *Con-*

gress should enact general provisions allowing a company to reduce risk through a method or approach other than that prescribed by regulation if the company can demonstrate that the new approach would bring about the same or greater degree of risk reduction. Obviously, a proposal allowing such flexibility would have to be accompanied by appropriate safeguards and penalties for abuse.

SCIENCE AND PRIORITIES

Inadequate scientific knowledge handicaps almost every aspect of efforts to achieve sustainable development. Too little is known to identify confidently either the significant threats to sustainability or their solutions. *A major increase in environmental research is essential, perhaps on the order of tripling the proportion of U.S. government research funds allocated for the environment.*

Although sound policy and decisionmaking must be firmly (but not exclusively) grounded in the best available scientific and technical information, this is often not the case. Economic and political considerations may overwhelm scientific information. The available science may not be relevant to the policy decisions to be made. Additionally, scientific knowledge may be available but not communicated in a usable form to policymakers.

The amount of evidence needed for scientific consensus is much greater than that needed to take policy actions. If governmental action were to require scientific certainty as a prerequisite, very few actions would ever be taken. Some dissenting scientists almost always can be found; some doubts can be raised about even the best-established scientific "fact." The policymaker must continuously weigh the amount of scientific evidence available to support action versus the potential consequences of not taking action. For the policymaker, unlike the scientist, waiting for further evidence is tantamount to deciding not to act.

Inverted Priorities. The clearest evidence that science is not a dominant factor in current environmental policymaking is the policy priorities as expressed by the budgets of EPA and the other federal environmental agencies. Problems that scientists rate as most important (including habitat destruction, loss of biological diversity, stratospheric ozone depletion, global climate change, indoor air pollution, and worker exposure to chemicals in industry and agriculture) receive the fewest resources, while those that scientists rate as less important (such as oil spills and groundwater pollution from waste sites) receive the highest priority.

Risk Communication. The reasons for the disparity between scientists' priorities and those of policymakers lie primarily in the realm of public opinion. This, in turn, involves the media, which influence the public, and Congress, which is influenced both by the media and public opinion and which in turn influences the executive branch and the states. All these influences are to some degree reciprocal. The failure of scientific opinion to influence national priorities is less a failure to communicate with policymakers than a failure to communicate with the public. If environmental priorities are to be based more on risk reduction than they now are, risk communication must be improved dramatically.

Both scientists and decisionmakers must learn how to communicate scientific knowledge, especially about risk, to nonexperts. If communication does not improve, government priorities will continue to be based on faulty assumptions about the risks presented by various environmental problems. Low-risk problems will continue to be a high priority while high-risk problems will continue to be neglected.

The government should give high priority to efforts to narrow the gap between public perceptions of risk and expert evaluations of risk. These efforts should include promoting citizen participation.

Communication between the experts and the public should be a dialogue. The public includes concepts in its definition of risk that scientists do not necessarily consider but that decisionmakers must address—such as whether a risk is undertaken voluntarily and whether it is catastrophic or incremental (e.g., plane crashes versus automobile accidents). Safety is not the only goal: society is also concerned about inhumanity and about personal and property rights that pollution invades or violates. Although the public needs to be more knowledgeable about certain risks, experts also need to broaden their concept of how to define risk.

Regulatory Decisionmaking. Decisionmaking about specific environmental regulations is another area where communication between scientists and policymakers is both important and deficient. One problem is that cancer risk has been emphasized above all other risks. In many regulatory decisions, cancers are the only type of risk considered, and the number of cancer cases avoided is the only benefit of regulatory action counted.

The reasons for the emphasis on cancer are both political and methodological. Politically, it is relatively easy for the public to respond to the risk of cancer. Most people know someone who has had cancer, and cancer is consistently at or near the top of the list of most dreaded diseases. Decisionmakers do not have to explain the benefits of avoiding cancer cases as they would have to explain the benefits of preserving wetlands or reducing neurological disorders. In terms of methodology, techniques for quantifying cancer risk are better developed than they are for other risks, and techniques for assigning dollar values to the risks are more accepted.

The number of cancer cases avoided is indeed an important benefit of some environmental regulatory actions. But for many (perhaps most) decisions, other benefits are more important. Moreover, the narrow focus on cancer can preclude regulatory actions that would have other kinds of benefits.

In the 1990s, two changes are likely to broaden the focus of environmental health concerns beyond cancer. The first is the growing understanding that a range of adverse health effects—immune system impairment, neurological disorders, birth defects, hormonal changes—are probably due in part to exposure to some environmental contaminants. In some cases these effects can occur at exposure levels below those associated with cancer or can be due to exposure to noncarcinogens.

The second factor is the awareness of new types of ecological problems that are regional or global in scale and that can have serious health consequences. Depletion of the stratospheric ozone layer is the prototypical and currently the most important of these problems. It involves the breakdown of a basic mechanism in the natural world as a result of human activity. The health consequences of this ecological breakdown include an estimated 1.6 million additional cases of eye cataracts and 300,000 more cases of skin cancer annually by the turn of the century, as well as a worsening of the danger from infectious diseases, including AIDS. As more is learned about the effects of such ecological changes, the line between ecological and health problems will become increasingly blurred.

Environmental scientists and health scientists must work together to recognize common sources of risk and both the environmental and the health benefits of risk reduction. Currently, environmental health scientists publish in different journals, use different jargon, attend different meetings, receive funding from different sources, and train in different departments. EPA, the National Science Foundation, and the National Institutes of Health should support interdisciplinary training programs. Both EPA and the National Research Council have proposed a risk assessment paradigm for ecological risk assessment that is analogous to the paradigm developed for environmental health risks.

The quality and timeliness of the scientific information used in regulatory decisionmaking is another major problem. Regulators often do not use the most up-to-date information because efforts to reach any major regulatory decision are so costly in terms of time, money, and political resources that decisionmakers are very reluctant to reopen questions even if new scientific findings seem to warrant reconsideration. On the other hand, government officials may also react to new risk findings with undue haste, failing to wait for adequate scientific confirmation or to consider other relevant information, especially if the public and Congress demand action.

New Partnerships. Decisionmakers and scientists must form a new working relationship. The relationship must be based on the recognition by decisionmakers that good science is at the heart of good policy; in the words of EPA Administrator William K. Reilly, in defining the problems to be solved and ways to solve them, "science . . . is really all we have." At the same time, scientists wishing to be involved in the policy process must listen to questions that policymakers want answered and make deliberate efforts to inject scientific results into the policy process.

Policymakers can foster good science by ensuring that all scientific evidence that plays a significant part in regulatory or policy decisions has undergone formal peer review—that is, a review of the methods and findings of a scientific study by scientists who are specialists in the area but who have not been involved in the research under review. Peer review is the primary mechanism by which the scientific community assesses the quality of research. *Public officials can improve their relations with the scientific community and also protect themselves from making decisions based on poor science if they routinely utilize the peer review process.*

Another important element of the partnership should be a mutual effort by scientists and policymakers to make the research agenda more relevant to future policy decisions. Time and again, research needed to make a decision has not been performed even though the need for the research could have been anticipated years in advance. We are not speaking here about the balance between research oriented to government regulatory needs and other types of research. We are talking about the timeliness and relevance of research done to support regulation.

Most environmental effects take longer than four years to become manifest. Knowing whether current policies are adequate depends on projections of at least one or two decades; however, nowhere in the U.S. government is this done. Several existing and potential mechanisms could help make the research agenda more relevant, significantly improve priority-setting, and help in formulating and implementing the National Environmental Strategy we described in Chapter 5.

EPA or the Department of the Environment should establish an office for long-range forecasting, and CEQ, working closely with state and federal environmental agencies, should issue periodic reports articulating 5- and 10-year environmental quality goals with specific and measurable national, state, and international objectives.

The model provided by the Netherlands is instructive (see Chapter 5). The Dutch government commissioned a long-range look at environmental conditions in 1981. This study revealed that most current policies would result in major deterioration of environmental conditions over the long run. As a result of the forecasting report, the Netherlands changed a number of its national policies.

Several U.S. states have issued environmental plans, such as "Washington 2010." However, there is no comprehensive *national* approach—like the National Environmental Strategy that we have recommended.

Additionally, a set of environmental goals and measurable objectives against which to evaluate program performance would greatly enhance the usefulness of strategic plans and of forecasting. To be most useful, goals must be quantitative and relate to actual environmental conditions rather than to administrative or legal measures. A useful model of this type of goal-setting is *Healthy People 2000*, a report issued by the U.S. Public Health Service. For goal-setting to be effective, systems must be in place to determine whether the goals are being met and to evaluate the effectiveness of programs.

MONITORING AND EVALUATION

Monitoring environmental conditions and evaluating environmental programs are as necessary for informed public participation in environmental decisions as they are for governmental decisions. Yet although monitoring and evaluation are basic functions, they are often neglected.

Monitoring involves five interrelated steps: design (what is to be monitored, why, and how), data collection, quality assurance, analysis, and reporting. Each step is essential. Collected data are worthless if their quality and validity cannot be assured. Data are almost never useful until they are analyzed; analysis converts numbers into information. Finally, information itself is not useful unless it is reported to the intended audience in a form that the audience can understand and use.

Environmental monitoring can be done for several purposes: to aid research, to provide a service (such as weather forecasting or reporting of groundwater levels), or to enhance enforcement of pollution control laws.

Evaluation, both of environmental conditions and of the performance of particular programs, is another major purpose potentially served by monitoring activities. Evaluation has been badly neglected, in part because no politically important groups support the collection and analysis of evaluation data. The public cannot know whether water quality in the United States is getting better or worse or whether an air pollution program is reducing urban smog because finding the answers has not been in anybody's interest. Moreover, monitoring can be costly and must be continued for an extended period before the findings are useful. Therefore, collecting and analyzing data often comes at the expense of other activities.

"Improved coordination" is a standard recommendation for good government, but in no area is there a greater need for coordination than in environmental monitoring. When a federal program wants to collect data, it usually establishes a new monitoring network. It often does not ask whether the data are already being collected by some other program or whether closely related data that are being collected could be used

instead. In part, lack of coordination exists because of bureaucratic possessiveness—reluctance to leave essential parts of a program in the hands of an outside program or agency.

Some of the lack of coordination results from the absence of institutional mechanisms to facilitate it. For example, because there is no central source of information about what environmental data are being collected, there is no place to find out whether other data exist that might obviate the need for a new collection effort. Significantly, the environment is almost the only major policy area that does not have a central statistical unit such as the Bureau of Labor Statistics, the National Center for Health Statistics, and similar offices that provide essential functions in their respective areas.

A Center for Environmental Statistics should be established in the Department of the Environment. The center, working closely with CEQ and other agencies, should produce regular reports on environmental conditions and trends.

EPA recently initiated an effort to create a center that (among its other tasks) would serve as a clearinghouse for environmental data. The center we propose would not collect data but would serve as a central reference concerning which agencies or organizations possess what data. Its reports would utilize data from other sources, such as EPA's Environmental Monitoring and Assessment Program (EMAP), the U.S. Geological Survey's National Ambient Water Quality Assessment, and various NOAA centers as well as the Toxicology and Environmental Health Program of the National Library of Medicine.

The Center for Environmental Statistics would have three short-term tasks: maintaining a directory of sources of environmental data, issuing an annual report on environmental quality, and doing special analyses that involve more than one data base. NEPA now assigns the reporting function to CEQ, which, using data supplied by other agencies, has attempted to report annually on environmental conditions. However, CEQ has never had enough staff to fulfill this role adequately. (EPA estimates that performing this work would take about 30 to 40 people—equal to CEQ's current total staff.)

Data from the center would be utilized by the long-range forecasting office discussed earlier. Over the longer run, we envision the center playing a key role in the goal-setting and progress-measuring aspects of the National Environmental Strategy.

An environmentally literate public also needs access to regular reports on environmental conditions so that it can make intelligent judgments about the seriousness of environmental problems and know whether expenditures are actually producing improvements in environmental quality. That said, the dangers and pitfalls of undertaking functions such as those contemplated for the Center for Environmental Statistics must be recognized so they may be avoided. The major danger is the poor quality of many environmental data. Manipulation, transfer, or storage of data almost never improves their quality and often makes matters worse because (among other problems) key caveats are lost or numbers misprinted. Thus, the center could inadvertently contribute to the poor quality of data or, perhaps worse, communicate erroneous conclusions to the public because of a failure to understand the limitations or characteristics of the data being used. Great care and diligence are necessary to avoid these problems.

Moving the focus "upstream" from remediation to prevention, committing to the integration of environmental programs, and collecting data are important not only for abating pollution but also for protecting habitats and natural systems within them. As shown in the concluding chapter of this report, sustainable development depends virtually on careful management of land and protection of biological diversity and ecosystems.

CHAPTER NINE

HABITATS FOR HUMANS AND OTHER SPECIES

**We envision an American landscape that sustains
natural systems, maximizes biological diversity,
and uplifts the human spirit.**

❖

**Environmentally sensitive management of public and
private land is essential to achieving environmental
goals and economic growth over the long term.**

The more people learn about natural habitats, the more they understand their overwhelming dependence and effect on their surroundings. Throughout history, people have attempted to shape nature to accommodate human needs. These efforts were originally intended to protect individuals and communities from the ravages of the natural environment. Now the situation is reversed: human alteration of natural habitats threatens natural systems and, in turn, humankind itself.

Human beings everywhere must fully appreciate that they are part of nature. Equipped with this awareness, humanity can—and, in our view, will—take steps to preserve and restore natural ecosystems and work to create environments that are sustainable and satisfying. Land-use management is a key tool to this end.

LAND USE

When Europeans first settled North America, the New World was viewed as a frightening and boundless wilderness. Taming this wilderness required government incentives and new notions of private land ownership. Thus, laws such as the Homestead Act and the 1872 Mining Act virtually gave away publicly owned lands and their resources in order to encourage expansion and development, and the Fifth Amendment to the Constitution prohibits governmental taking of private property without just compensation.

These and other policies have succeeded in almost wiping out the American wilderness. More than 90 percent of the nation's original forests have been lost since the first Europeans settled here. Although America's forest coverage has increased in recent years, the new growth does not replace the native habitats or species that have been lost. Ninety-nine percent of the tall-grass prairies are gone. Less than 6 percent of the original 215 million acres of wetlands remain in the coterminous United States, and wetlands continue to be lost at a rate of about 300,000 acres each year. Approximately 500 plant and animal species are known to have become extinct in the United States since the European arrival.

Meanwhile, sprawling housing developments, shopping centers, highways, and myriad other developments have proceeded virtually unfettered by any sense of respect for the environment and humankind's relation to it. As a result, pollution from nonpoint sources continues to grow and is increasingly difficult to control; biological diversity is destroyed as habitats are fragmented and eliminated; sprawl development blights the landscape and precludes cost-effective and environmentally beneficial means of providing transportation and other services; and inner cities at the core of metropolitan areas increasingly are home only to people who have been abandoned as hopeless by the rest of U.S. society.

Land-use regulation in the United States has been characterized by two main features. First, the authority to regulate land in the public interest is generally vested in the states, which in turn have delegated most of their regulatory power to local governments. Second, land has been considered a commodity, the quintessence of private property. Although government-imposed limits on land use have been legally sanctioned for many years, a large number of people consider any government interference with private land use a threat to individual liberty and the capitalist system.

Government regulation of private land use is, in fact, an integral part of the American tradition. As one history of U.S. urban development notes, "all of the colonial cities and towns were planned communities in origin; the idea that their growth might be shaped by individuals' interests in real estate speculation was to emerge only slowly." What has changed in recent years is that land regulation has increasingly moved beyond urban areas, where many of its benefits are obvious, to natural areas such as wetlands and beaches, where the need for regulation depends more on an understanding of and respect for environmental relationships.

Both the legal division of powers and strong feelings about private property suggest that efforts to regulate land use must involve state and local governments. The federal government may play a role (as it does, for example, under the Coastal Zone Management Act or the Clean Water Act), but its role should be primarily that of a partner with states.

Specific statutes have been enacted at federal, state, and local levels to protect particular resources, including wetlands, prime agricultural land, historic buildings and sites, endangered species, scenic river corridors, and high-risk areas such as certain coastal zones. Systems of land planning and zoning have been established at local levels, especially in the more developed segments of the country, in an effort to guide land development.

These efforts, however, have not eliminated the undesirable effects of the land development process. Issue-specific statutes have by their nature produced only limited and fragmentary protection. Zoning and planning have often been merely a system for regulating the rate of destruction of the land and its natural values instead of a means to ensure the maintenance of the highest values of this country's natural resource base.

Even these rudimentary systems of resource protection, however, have increasingly come under attack as an unconstitutional interference with private property rights. Thus, the effort to guide and, where appropriate, limit the development of natural resources has met with a chilling influence. The courts are increasingly seen as reluctant to support measures to control land development. This trend cannot continue if the rich bounty of the American landscape is to nurture the well-being of present and future generations and if humans are to strike an accord that respects the survival rights of the plants and animals with which they share the Earth.

A new direction must be found. It must be based on a restatement of fundamental values. First, a broader understanding of the nature of private property ownership is needed. The public has a legitimate interest in preventing uses of private property that can harm the natural resource base. Second, America needs to articulate clearly the values of land, or property, that are of public interest and thus can transcend property owners' personal interests. *Qualities of the land on which the public well-being depends, such as the protection of water supplies or the maintenance of biological diversity, are interests of vital importance to society, and government actions to protect these public interests should be deemed legitimate.*

The federal government has both a direct and an indirect impact on land use, apart from its management of public lands (which will be dealt with shortly). Its direct impact is in the form of such actions as grants for water and sewer lines, highways, and construction or closing military facilities, where effects on land use often are only an afterthought. Indirect impacts are in the form of federal cooperation with states in land-use activities (such as the federal government's cooperation with Maryland to address nonpoint pollution entering the Chesapeake Bay). Both types of impact should be acknowledged so that the overall environmental effects of land use receive more attention.

Federal cooperation with the states on land-use matters has been mostly obscure and of low priority. The tone was set in 1971 when the Land Use Policy, Planning, and Assistance Act was submitted to Congress. The focus of this bill was not federal land-use planning but rather federal assistance to state planning efforts. Confusion over the bill's purpose probably explains both Congress' failure to pass it and some lasting suspicion about whether Congress recognizes a federal role of any type in state or local land-use management. The time has come to return to this issue because in many instances the protection of environmental quality hinges on adequate land-use planning and regulation.

In our view, there is a logical *quid pro quo* in the relationship between the federal government and the states with regard to land use that has been partially realized in the provisions of the Coastal Zone Management Act. If the states provide an adequate legal and administrative mechanism for environmental protection and for local land-use planning, they will be helping to fulfill national goals for the environment. In return, the federal government should agree to abide by state

and local plans (unless there is a conflict and the federal agency proposing the action demonstrates that the action will benefit the environment or other national interest), thereby helping states and localities
control the land-use effects of federal actions. The federal government
should consider other incentives to encourage state land-use planning,
including providing funding for state planning.

Congress should enact legislation to:

— **support state and local land-use planning by identifying and establishing planning criteria to provide for
balanced use of lands, to protect environmental quality, and to provide for economic and other social purposes; and**

— **ensure that any federal actions are consistent with
and meet state or local plans that accord with the federal criteria, and provide financial support for development and implementation of the state plans.**

Planning criteria should include protecting environmentally sensitive areas, including watersheds, aquifers, and wetlands; maintaining
biodiversity; continuing the productivity of agricultural land; ensuring
that sites for economic activity are appropriate and available; encouraging energy efficiency; and protecting sites of natural beauty and of historic and cultural value.

The federal government has a long tradition of working with the
states in the land-use area. Statutes such as the Coastal Zone Management Act and the Surface Mining and Reclamation Act contain elements of such cooperation in land management. The Intermodal
Surface Transportation and Efficiency Act passed in 1991 reflects a new
willingness on the part of the federal government to give the states
greater flexibility and control over important infrastructure decisions.
*Land-use management that protects the environmental interest of this and
future generations must be carried out in a partnership involving the several levels of government that characterize the federal system.*

A notable exception to the key state and local land-use role is the vast acreage owned by the federal government itself. The federal government owns almost a third of the total land in the United States and more than half of the land in the western states. These public lands support habitats for myriad varieties of life; they contain an enormous supply of renewable and nonrenewable resources; and they provide cultural enrichment through their majestic beauty and historic significance.

Regardless of which agency manages them, the federal lands are held in public trust for the entire nation. Nevertheless, some groups have acted as if the federal lands were the property of particular users or commercial interests. *Federal lands are the property of all citizens, and their management should be based on a land ethic, sound principles of sustainability, and a strong sense of duty to future generations.*

Unfortunately, many federal holdings are not managed on a sustainable basis. Most federal land is managed according to the concept of multiple use, where the productivity of the land is maintained by ensuring the continual production of renewable resources, including recreation, grazing, watershed, timber, and fish and wildlife, as well as the extraction of nonrenewable resources such as oil, natural gas, coal, and hardrock minerals. Although multiple use is not inherently unsustainable, the delicate balance between various uses often has been disrupted by land managers who have placed excessive emphasis on resources (such as timber, grazing, or mineral extraction) that are perceived to be of economic benefit, particularly to private interests.

We are not opposed to multiple use. However, the notion must be redefined to incorporate the principle of sustainability. Laws should make clear that sustainability is the precondition for all other management choices. Statutory and administrative changes are necessary both to bring about sustainable management and to ensure that the public receives a fair return on any use of its lands.

Management on public lands that is now based on multiple use should be made compatible with sustainability.

Sustainable management of federal lands has been handicapped by the number and diversity of agencies exercising management control. The Bureau of Land Management, the Forest Service, the

Federal/State Cooperation in Land-Use Planning: The Coastal Zone Management Act

Congress enacted the Coastal Zone Management Act of 1972 (CZMA) (16 USC 1452) "to preserve, protect, develop, and where possible, to restore, or enhance, the resources of the Nation's coastal zone for this and succeeding generations" (Section 301 (a)). The CZMA was designed to establish general national goals for improved coastal management by developing individual state and territorial programs that address both national concerns and local needs.

The act provides federal funding for states to develop and implement comprehensive controls and management plans for land and water use. These controls and plans are subject to federal approval from the National Oceanic and Atmospheric Administration's Office of Ocean and Coastal Resource Management. An additional nonfinancial incentive is the CZMA's consistency provision, which holds that once a state's management program receives federal approval, all federal actions that directly affect the coastal zone must, to the maximum extent possible, be consistent with the state's approved plan.

Through FY1992, 29 states and territories had developed approved coastal management programs. Between 1974 and 1992, almost $61 million in federal grant funds were given to coastal states and territories to develop these programs, and almost $465 million in federal funds were made available to implement them. Most of these funds have been devoted to improved legal and administrative mechanisms for better government decisionmaking (e.g., permit simplification efforts, land-use plan preparation) and for natural resource protection (e.g., water quality studies, habitat protection projects).

Nevertheless, the CZMA's procedures for grant-making, performance reports, and program evaluation have made it difficult to assess how the individual state programs are collectively addressing national goals. As a result, the 1990 reauthorization amendments established the Coastal Zone Enhancement Grants Program (Section 309), which identifies eight areas for state program improvement. The Enhancement Grants Program is a concerted effort to change the state perspective on federal grants for coastal protection from one of entitlement based on state needs to one of meeting national goals. Through Section 309 and other provisions, the 1990 reauthorization reflects a rekindled interest in shifting the CZMA toward a state/federal partnership designed to address critical coastal land-use concerns.

National Park Service, and the Fish and Wildlife Service are among those responsible for large portions of the public lands. These agencies often have different mandates and overlapping jurisdictions. Coordinating their actions is analogous to coordinating the actions of diverse private owners. There is currently no system for coordinating the management of federal lands even when such lands are adjacent to each other and are part of a single ecosystem. The result is habitat fragmentation and loss of biological diversity.

The President should issue an executive order establishing an interagency policy committee on federal lands to identify and establish priorities and to coordinate the management of environmentally significant federal lands.

Sustainable management is further hampered by what can only be called the perverse subsidies relating to the use of natural resources. In many instances the government does not receive market value or even recover its investment in managing the resources and facilitating private-sector resource extraction. Such underpricing subsidizes and encourages the overuse of resources and the destruction of habitats.

The principles of sustainable development and fair return to the public are closely related. As discussed in Chapter 3, getting the price right is key to ensuring sustainability. A fair return means a return based on a price that includes social as well as private costs. Applying sustainable development and fair return principles also would mean important changes in federal management of timber, oil and gas leases, mining, and grazing.

Subsidies and below-market arrangements that encourage unsustainable use of natural resources on public lands should be eliminated.

Below-Cost Timber Sales. To make sustainable development possible, current federal timber harvesting policies must be revamped and below-cost timber sales eliminated. The annual costs of timber harvesting, which include road construction, reforestation, administration, and other services, have consistently exceeded the annual revenue raised by the federal government from timber sales in seven of the nine National Forest regions. Over the past decade, federal expenditures in three regions (the

Rocky Mountain, Northeast, and Intermountain regions) have exceeded gross receipts by a factor of three.

Pricing timber below cost is economically inefficient and encourages unsustainable harvesting. Current timber practices will have severe environmental and economic effects, especially in the Pacific Northwest where logging at the current rate will obliterate much of the nation's remaining old-growth forests and cause significant ecological damage and loss of cultural heritage. Subsidies allow or even encourage the harvest of timber on steep, rocky terrains that require extensive road systems, where steep slopes make reforestation difficult and geography increases the probability of extreme runoff, erosion, and sedimentation. Moreover, while openings created by timber harvesting may provide habitat for some "edge" species, most of the forest species thought to be in jeopardy or declining require large, uninterrupted forest tracts to survive. *As a first step in attaining a sustainable yield, the Forest Service should be required to set genuinely sustainable targets for timber sales in its Resources Planning Act Program.*

It is important to note that despite below-cost timber sales, the timber industry has experienced substantial job losses because of labor-saving technological improvements in logging, milling, and transportation; the shift toward regions of higher productivity; and broad economic factors. Current practices have contributed to the development of timber-dependent communities that lack the resources to diversify and develop other long-term employment opportunities. Clearly, every effort should be made to mitigate the impact of eliminating timber subsidies on local and regional economies. Steps should be taken to anticipate and avoid economic dislocations and to stimulate adjustment assistance and job retraining.

Mining Subsidies. The 1872 Mining Act is another impediment to the sustainable management of public lands and resources. This act contains many anachronistic provisions written when development of U.S. mining resources was considered the the most important of all possible uses of federal lands. The 1872 Act grants prospectors the right to mine and sell public minerals without paying any fees or royalties except for a nominal $100 annual expenditure to develop the claim. In addition, land-holding claims can be patented and purchased for merely $2.50 to $5.00 per acre. The Mining Act's free-access principle for hardrock mining on public lands invites abuse and fails to recognize the increasing importance of environmental protection and strategies for sustainable land management. The absence of any royalty or license fees amounts to giving away publicly owned natural resources without regard for the environmental costs associated with mineral development.

The 1872 Mining Act should be amended to create federal leasing programs that require environmental protection and a fair-market return for publicly owned resources. The amendments should provide the Bureau of Land Management, the Forest Service, and other federal agencies with clear authority to prohibit any mining on public lands that causes significant environmental damage. All mining and reclamation plans should be subject to approval of the applicable agency's environmental protection guidelines, which should include strict regulation of reclamation techniques and liability provisions to cover restoration costs. The legislation should also ensure a fair economic return to the federal government by imposing a surface-use fee and a royalty based on a fair percentage of the value of the mining claim. Federal agencies also should have authority to impose penalties for violations of regulations; if destructive activity does not cease, they should be able to eject miners (subject to judicial review).

Grazing Fees. Private herders use a large number of federal acres to graze sheep and cattle. Historically, the charges for grazing on federal lands were significantly below the costs for grazing on private land. Although grazing fees have been increased in recent years, they still tend to fall below market levels and thus encourage overgrazing, which has degraded the land. The public subsidizes the grazers as well as unsustainable practices that destroy public land. *Federal grazing fees should be increased to reflect their market value and to achieve a sustainable level of grazing on public lands.*

PROTECTING BIODIVERSITY

Humans now have the power to pollute the world on a global scale. Human developments have disturbed and fragmented natural habitats, many of which are critical to support biodiversity. Many natural habitats that once supported biodiversity have already been lost; no ecosystem has escaped human impact. Humankind is only beginning to comprehend that its actions significantly affect biodiversity and that protection of biodiversity is a human responsibility. Left unchecked, human activities could eventually destroy the very habitats on which humankind depends.

Biodiversity can be viewed at three basic levels: genetic or within-species; species diversity, or the numbers and frequencies of species; and ecosystem diversity, or the variety of organism communities in their natural habitats. (Some experts add a fourth level: landscape or regional biodiversity.) Different policies are usually aimed at different levels.

The effects of human activities on all levels of biodiversity have been considerable, although the full extent is not understood. Paul Ehrlich and Edward O. Wilson, two of the foremost experts on the subject, state that "because the life of the planet remains mostly unexplored at the species and infraspecies levels, systematists [classifiers of species] do not know the species diversity of the total world fauna and flora to the nearest order of magnitude." There may be 10 million species, or there may be 100 million. Nevertheless, Ehrlich and Wilson go on to estimate that if the current rate of clearing of tropical forests continues, one-quarter or more of the species on Earth could be eliminated within 50 years.

Such problems are not limited to the tropics. Over the past 18 years, the Fish and Wildlife Service has listed approximately 700 species as threatened or endangered and has identified over 6,000 species and subspecies as candidates for that status in the United States. Many of these species are found in wetlands, mature forests, and native grasslands—habitats that are under severe pressure from large-scale and ongoing human intrusion. In the nation's most biologically diverse states—Hawaii, California, Texas, and Florida—and elsewhere, whole communities of plants and animals are threatened. For example, Florida's Everglades ecosystem is in imminent danger of disappearing, and the Northwest's old-growth ecosystem is a major and imperiled source of controversy.

Global environmental problems also threaten biodiversity. If global warming occurs more rapidly than natural systems can adapt, some species will be destroyed and many ecosystems drastically altered. For example, rising sea levels would submerge many saltwater wetlands. In addition, there is evidence that the phytoplankton communities that are an integral part of the Antarctic ecosystem may be harmed by the increase in ultraviolet radiation reaching the Earth as a result of stratospheric ozone loss.

The United States has no clearly defined national policy or coherent program for maintaining biodiversity. Federal and state government agencies and programs that affect biodiversity are not coordinated, and at times they conflict. Although park, wildlife refuge, and natural heritage programs each pursue separate conservation missions, forestry, water resources, and economic development programs often adversely affect natural habitats and the biodiversity that depends on them. Similarly, owners and managers of private lands in the United States frequently engage in agricultural, commercial, and industrial activities with little understanding of how they might be affecting the biodiversity of their lands or of adjacent habitats.

Protection and enhancement of the native biodiversity and important ecosystems of the United States should be a national goal, and the federal government should institute a national policy strategy aimed at conserving biodiversity.

The focus of this strategy should be linking habitat protection with ecosystem management, recognizing the legitimacy of both natural and economic uses of land, and applying a range of methods and techniques for managing public and private land and water resources to maintain biodiversity. The biodiversity strategy should be an element of the National Environmental Strategy outlined in Chapter 5.

The emphasis of U.S. biodiversity policy should be on protecting habitats as well as on saving individual species and should be integrated into land-use planning and management. Preserving and strengthening the federal Endangered Species Act (ESA) is essential; however, the protection and enhancement of native biodiversity should focus primarily on preventing the further fragmentation of natural habitats and ensuring the long-term maintenance and enhancement of functioning ecosystems. While at times it will be necessary to save a particular species, protecting biodiversity one species at a time is inefficient and difficult. To the extent possible, the focus should be on saving ecosystems, for without its ecosystem, a species cannot survive.

California is experimenting with a program that focuses on habitats instead of specific endangered species. On the national level, an ecosystem approach should involve a concerted effort to mesh federal land acquisition and management programs and Habitat Conservation Plans (HCPs) under the ESA, with priorities based on a National Inventory of Biodiversity and with information collected under the ESA.

Congress should enact legislation requiring a National Inventory of Biodiversity for public and private lands and establishing a mechanism for disseminating this information to planners and resource managers.

A National Inventory of Biodiversity would be a major tool in expanding the endangered species focus to include habitats. It would help provide better knowledge of the distribution and identity of species and ecosystems within the United States. This information could help reduce costly mistakes, such as assuming that a species is endangered when it is not or that it is unique to a particular area when it is found in other areas. More important, such an inventory would permit species and ecosystem protection to be dealt with *before* there is a proposed development or some other crisis and before options are foreclosed by extinction.

The Nature Conservancy, a private organization, has already compiled extensive biodiversity inventories on a state-by-state basis. Both Canada and Australia have national biodiversity inventories, and Costa Rica is compiling one. "Gap analysis," a method for determining which areas are richest in biodiversity and which ones are inadequately protected, is another way to focus the nation's habitat management to protect biodiversity (see box).

The extent to which the ESA has interfered with development or resource extraction generally has been exaggerated. For example, under section 7 (which requires federal agencies undertaking actions likely to jeopardize the continued existence of a listed species to consult with the Fish and Wildlife Service [FWS] or National Marine Fisheries Service [NMFS], which must issue a "jeopardy opinion" if either service determines that the action endangers a species) from 1987 to 1991, FWS conducted 71,560 informal and 2,000 formal consultations and issued only 350 jeopardy opinions; NMFS conducted 248 formal consultations and issued only 3 opinions. Of these, only 19 projects were ultimately blocked, canceled, or terminated due to section 7. Although the United States should broaden its biodiversity policy to habitats and ecosystems, the Endangered Species Act will continue to be a crucial element in the national biodiversity strategy.

A major problem with the ESA is lack of funding. Inadequate resources have impeded both the listing of species as endangered or

Gap Analysis

Gap analysis is premised on the concept that the best way to protect biodiversity is to preserve native species in their natural habitat. It attempts to present researchers and managers with an overview of how effectively biodiversity is being protected. Gap analysis uses the geographic information system (GIS) capabilities of digital map overlay to compile a single data base from satellite images of topography and vegetation, land ownership and management records, and records of native species and community occurrences. The completed maps encompass the variety and variability of natural vegetation, native species, eco-regions, existing reserves, and land ownership, and thus provide an indication of which areas are the "richest" in terms of biological diversity—and which areas are inadequately protected. The maps are compiled on a broad scale to move management decisions away from a more traditional species-by-species approach and toward a landscape-level assessment of conservation efforts that allows for the protection of biodiversity at all levels of activity.

Although not a substitute for a national biodiversity inventory, gap analysis provides direction for managers who must set priorities for land acquisition. Because the ranges of endangered species are usually overlaid on maps, gap analysis helps show where potential conflicts exist. Thus, managers may target limited acquisition funds on the landscapes that are most important from a biodiversity perspective.

Gap analysis is under way in over 30 states. The Idaho Cooperative Fish and Wildlife Research Unit just completed its state's gap analysis in fiscal year 1992. Information from Idaho's gap analysis already has been used to develop four proposals for new national parks. With a cost of approximately $300,000 per state, researchers hope that an annual budget of $4 million will allow gap analyses for the entire United States to be completed by 1998.

threatened (about 6,000 species are candidates for listing under the ESA) and the development of HCPs.

Congress should increase appropriations for the Endangered Species Act with particular support for Habitat Conservation Plans.

The HCP mechanism of the ESA was created to address the problem of otherwise lawful activities incidentally and unintentionally killing or harming a species listed under the ESA. HCPs are long-term plans to promote conservation of listed species; landowners who agree to implement them are permitted to continue activities that incidentally take a small number of protected species where such losses are offset by the plan. HCPs can address the effects of proposed activities on single or multiple species over small or large areas of land. The Fish and Wildlife Service has formally approved seven HCPs, and more than 20 are in various stages of development.

The ESA also suffers from a lack of scientific information. Research on ecology has been seriously neglected. Although the National Aeronautics and Space Administration, NOAA, the Forest Service, the National Science Foundation, the Fish and Wildlife Service, EPA, and a number of other agencies sponsor some ecological research, nowhere in the federal government is there an agency that has central responsibility for improving ecological knowledge. In Chapter 8 we called for a major increase in funding for environmental research. *A dramatic rise in ecological research is also needed to assess ecological conditions, identify threats, and craft solutions.*

As with other programs discussed in this report, implementation of the ESA is weakened by the lack of coordination among programs. Coordination among the ESA and the approximately 30 other federal laws relating to biodiversity conservation is also necessary, especially if policy is to expand to focus on habitats.

Federal Water Rights: We stated in Chapter 3 that water subsidies to already subsidized crops should be eliminated. These subsidies drain the nation's financial resources and encourage agricultural development in unsuitable places, can lead to excessive energy consumption, and deprive wildlife of water that may be crucial to their survival.

Another practice that must change is the failure to assert federal water rights. In the Western states, the federal government holds reserved water rights that accompany federally owned land. Nevertheless, as water demand has increased, water flowing onto public lands has been diverted by upstream users, and fish and wildlife on the federal lands have been threatened because of the reduced in-stream flow. Some western states have laws protecting in-stream flows to protect riparian areas. *Federal land managers should aggressively assert federal reserved water rights to protect biodiversity on federal lands.*

The marine environment is often overlooked or neglected in discussions of the effects of human activity on ecosystems, but it is no less important and no less threatened than are many land areas. Oceans cover 71 percent of the Earth's surface and are home to an enormous diversity of life. Oceans also interact with the atmosphere to regulate the Earth's climatic systems.

Pressure on the Earth's marine ecosystems is increasing. Most of the world's population lives in coastal areas; nearly three-quarters are expected to live in coastal areas by the end of this century. In the United States, human population density in coastal counties is four times the average density; about 45 percent of the U.S. population lives in coastal counties (including the Great Lakes). Thus, coastal ecosystems are subject to greater pressures from human development than are any other systems.

Coral reefs are particularly vulnerable to pollution and other human-induced stresses. Approximately 30 percent of all coral reef cover in the Florida Keys has been lost since 1970. Many marine species are in decline or endangered, and commercially important fisheries are being exploited on an unsustainable basis. Crashes in the population of fish, marine mammals, seabirds, and invertebrates as well as chemical contamination of marine animals, loss of coral reefs, and increased frequency of red tides are all strong indicators of diminishing biodiversity and balance.

One attempt to mitigate the over-exploitation of marine life was embodied in the Magnuson Fisheries Management and Conservation Act. The Magnuson Act governs the maintenance of stocks of commercially valuable fish species in the United States. It was originally designed to provide a framework for ensuring that overfishing would not destroy valuable fisheries. It is seriously flawed, however, because the limits on allowable catches are set by regional boards dominated by the commercial fishing industry. In most cases, industry representatives have been unable to resist making short-term gains at the expense of long-term conservation of commercial species and have set catch limits at unsustainably high levels. *Therefore, a revised act should specify that catch limits be established by boards that include scientific experts and are not dominated by the fishing industry.*

The Magnuson Act should be significantly amended to provide better long-term protection for commercial fish species.

Many of the threats to the resources of the coastal environment result from the intense human occupation of the land adjacent to the water's edge. Development activities can cause pollution, especially of the type that is diffuse and therefore extremely hard to control. In addition, habitats such as marshes and mud flats can be substantially altered so that they no longer support a range of marine life. Most important marine species spend some critical period of their life-cycles in this edge environment, which gradually is being destroyed.

Increasingly, states have adopted a variety of land management systems that are designed to minimize these effects and to help ensure that only those development activities that are dependent on the water are located in coastal regions. These management systems generally operate through a mix of minimum performance standards for particular uses in combination with a planning process for locating development activities in the most environmentally appropriate areas. Usually state authorities set the minimum procedural and substantive objectives while specific plans and decisions are made at a more local level. There are many variations; Oregon, California, and Maryland provide instructive examples. *Virtually every coastal state faces a declining quality of its coastal environment in the face of growing population pressures, and these states need to adopt sound strategies to avoid the demise of their valuable coastal resources.*

Whether marine or terrestrial, the health of all life is interdependent. Human beings, as members of a species with the power to manipulate and destroy, would be wise to be aware of their actions and their long-range consequences. The narrow focus of exploitation for economic gain leads us toward goals that are simply not sustainable. Protection of the Earth's biodiversity is crucial for the survival of all life.

In shifting goals from exploitation to sustainability, it is also important to realize how little people really know about ecosystems, their interactions, and the broader context of global systems. The relative newness of the concepts of ecosystems and interactive global systems attests to this. Thus, "management" of ecosystems and the global environment may be unrealistic because people understand too little about how the Earth functions as a whole.

This lack of understanding should caution humanity to tread lightly. While human effects on the environment may not always be immediately apparent, people have had and will always have repercussions. Before acting, it is imperative to look at the big picture. By viewing human actions in their full context and living as sustainably as possible, present and future generations may be able to avoid the mistakes of the past.

WE ENVISION

This report has been guided by a positive vision of the future: a vision of what the United States can and should become in an era when the relationship of humans and nature is a central issue. We envision:

An America where public and private values and actions promote sustainable development

An America in which a new generation of technologies contributes to the conservation of resources and the protection of the environment

An America in which market prices and economic indicators reflect the full environmental and social costs of human activities

An America with an environmentally literate citizenry that has the knowledge, skills, and ethical values needed to achieve sustainable development

An America where leaders are committed to long-term environmental protection and to international leadership and cooperation in addressing the world's environmental problems

A world in which human numbers are stabilized, all people enjoy a decent standard of living through sustainable development, and the global environment is protected for future generations

An America in which energy is abundant, affordable, nonpolluting, and used efficiently

An America in which the entire life-cycle of a product is part of a strategy of waste reduction and pollution prevention

An American landscape that sustains natural systems, maximizes biological diversity, and uplifts the human spirit.

Our vision can become reality, but not unless hard decisions and difficult actions are taken. On one hand, if the nation drifts and fails to realize the importance of the environmental choices that lie before it, the consequences will range from serious to disastrous. If, on the other hand, the nation acts on the recommendations outlined in this report, it will launch itself on a path toward sustainable development and a better future for the Earth and all its inhabitants.

ADDITIONAL
COMMENTS

Robert M. White, joined by Lee M. Thomas: Increasing energy taxes to achieve environmental and other broad national economic objectives can be wise public policy if the social and economic consequences of such increases are well understood. Specific levels of increases, however, must rest on a base of analysis and data that clearly are beyond the scope of this Commission's work. Accordingly, while I agree with the objectives stated in this portion of the report, I disagree to the extent that the language of the report is construed as proposing any specific energy tax levels.

John E. Bryson: While I believe that gasoline and carbon taxes deserve serious consideration, I agree with Dr. White that the secondary consequences deserve fuller analysis than has been possible in this Commission. With respect to carbon dioxide emissions, I favor the no regrets policy proposed by, among others, the National Academy of Sciences in its 1991 report, *Policy Implications of Greenhouse Warming.* The country should take, at this time, those now-available and low-cost steps that are independently justified by sound economics as a reasonable insurance policy against the uncertain potential for global warming. Finally, I believe the report would be strengthened by focusing on source fuel efficiency, that is, on using the least total amount of energy to perform a given task. Efforts to achieve source fuel efficiency should be at the top of the nation's energy policy agenda.

NOTES TO TEXT

CHAPTER 1: THE GOAL OF SUSTAINABLE DEVELOPMENT

The World Commission on Environment and Development (WCED), chaired by Prime Minister Gro Harlem Brundtland, articulated the meaning and importance of sustainable development in its seminal report, *Our Common Future* (New York, N.Y.: Oxford University Press, 1987). Additional information about sustainable development can be found in *Agenda 21* (New York, N.Y.: United Nations, forthcoming); World Resources Institute, *World Resources 1992-93, A Guide to the Global Environment: Toward Sustainable Development* (New York, N.Y.: Oxford University Press, 1992); National Commission on America and the New World, *Changing Our Ways: America and the New World* (Washington, D.C.: Carnegie Endowment for International Peace, 1992); and the proceedings of the Centennial Symposium, "Earth '88: Changing Geographic Perspectives" (Washington, D.C.: National Geographic Society, 1988). Also, see Lester Brown, *Building a Sustainable Society* (New York, N.Y.: W.W. Norton, 1981); International Union for the Conservation of Nature and Natural Resources, World Wildlife Fund, United Nations Environment Programme, *Caring for the Earth: A Strategy for Sustainable Living* (Washington, D.C.: Island Press, 1991); and Stephan Schmidheiny with the Business Council for Sustainable Development, *Changing Course* (Cambridge, Mass.: MIT Press, 1992).

Characteristics of Technology for Sustainable Development

For a discussion of new technology, see George Heaton, Robert Repetto, and Rodney Sobin, *Transforming Technology: An Agenda for Sustainable Growth in the 21st Century* (Washington, D.C.: World Resources Institute, April 1991); George R. Heaton, Jr., Robert Repetto, and Rodney Sobin, *Backs to the Future: U.S. Government Policy Toward Environmentally Critical Technology* (Washington, D.C.: World Resources Institute, June 1992); James Gustave Speth, "EPA Must Help Lead an Environmental Revolution in Technology," *Environmental Law*, vol. 21 (1991), p. 1425; and James Gustave Speth, "The Greening of Technology," *The Washington Post*, November 20, 1988, p. D3.; and Jesse H. Ausubel and Hedy Sladovich, eds., *Technology and Environment* (Washington, D.C.: National Academy Press, 1989).

Obstacles to the Adoption of Environmentally Superior Technologies

For a fuller discussion on the difficulties facing the rapid diffusion of CFC-substitute technologies into developing and developed countries, see National Academy of Engineering, *Cross-Border Technology Transfer to Eliminate Ozone-Depleting Substances* (Washington, D.C.: National Academy Press, 1992).

For a discussion of regulatory impediments to technology development in the Clean Air Act, see David Harrison, Jr., and Paul R. Portney, "Making Ready for the Clean Air Act," *Regulation*, vol. 5 (March/April 1981), p. 24.

Encouraging the Development and Deployment of New Technologies

For a comprehensive analysis of reforms to remove regulatory obstacles and encourage the development and diffusion of environmentally superior technologies, see U.S. Environmental Protection Agency, Office of the Administrator, *Permitting and Compliance Policy: Barriers to U.S. Environmental Technology Innovation* (Washington, D.C.: EPA, 1991). New technologies and initiatives to promote them are also discussed in George R. Heaton, Jr., Robert Repetto, and Rodney Sobin, *Backs to the Future: U.S. Government Policy Toward*

Environmentally Critical Technology (Washington, D.C.: World Resources Institute, June 1992).

The U.S. Environmental Protection Agency has established the Technology Innovation Office within the Office of Solid Waste and Emergency Response to promote the most effective methods of cleaning up hazardous waste sites.

Information in the box on Japan's "New Earth 21" program can be found in Ministry of International Trade and Industry, "The New Earth 21: Action Program for the Twenty-First Century," and in Frederick S. Myers, "Japan Bids for Global Leadership in Clean Industry," *Science*, vol. 256 (May 22, 1992), pp. 1144-45.

For a more detailed breakdown of the resources devoted to environmental technology research and development, see Congressional Research Service, *Federal R&D in Environmental Technologies* (Washington, D.C.: Library of Congress, July 17, 1992).

For an analysis of federal environmental research and development programs and recommendations on how to strengthen these programs, see Carnegie Commission on Science, Technology, and Government, *Environmental Research and Development: Strengthening the Federal Infrastructure* (New York, N.Y.: Carnegie Commission on Science, Technology, and Government, December 1992).

Statistics given in the box on government-industry cooperation in technology development were drawn from the following sources: U.S. Department of Energy, *Clean Coal Technology Demonstration Program, Program Update 1990* (Washington, D.C.: DOE, February 1991), *Clean Coal Technology: A New Coal Era* (Washington, D.C.: DOE, November 1989), and a fact sheet produced by the U.S. Advanced Battery Consortium entitled "A Cooperative R&D Program for Electric Vehicle Advanced Batteries" (Washington, D.C.: DOE, 1991).

CHAPTER 3: ECONOMICS FOR SUSTAINABLE DEVELOPMENT

Market Mechanisms

For a more comprehensive discussion of the economic incentives available to promote environmental goals, see U.S. Environmental Protection Agency, Office of Policy, Planning, and Evaluation, *Economic Incentives: Options for Environmental Protection* (Washington, D.C.: EPA, 1991); Timothy E. Wirth and John Heinz, *Project 88:*

Harnessing Market Forces to Protect Our Environment (Washington, D.C.: Alliance to Save Energy, 1988); and Senator Timothy E. Wirth and Senator John Heinz, *Project 88: Round II Incentives for Action: Designing Market-Based Environmental Strategies* (Washington, D.C.: Alliance to Save Energy, 1991). Also, see Frederick R. Anderson et al., *Environmental Improvement through Economic Incentives* (Washington, D.C.: Resources for the Future, 1977), and Robert N. Stavins and Bradley W. Whitehead, "Dealing with Pollution: Market-based Incentives for Environmental Protection," *Environment* (September 1992), p. 7.

The emissions trading mechanism for sulfur dioxide in the 1990 Clean Air Act is expected to save society between $8.9 and $12.9 billion over the next 18 years (i.e., from 1993 to 2010), compared to what the same amount of control would have cost without a trading mechanism. See U.S. Environmental Protection Agency, Office of Atmospheric and Indoor Air Programs, Acid Rain Division, *Regulatory Impact Analysis of the Proposed Acid Rain Implementation Regulations* (prepared by ICF Incorporated for the EPA, September 16, 1991), pp. ES-6 and ES-7.

For an overview of the use of market mechanisms in the United States and Europe, see Organization for Economic Cooperation and Development, *Economic Instruments for Environmental Protection* (Paris: OECD, 1989).

Getting the Prices Right

The environmental and economic costs of "hidden" subsidies supporting automobile use are discussed in James J. MacKenzie, Roger C. Dower, and Donald D.T. Chen, *The Going Rate: What It Really Costs to Drive* (Washington, D.C.: World Resources Institute, June 1992).

The elasticity of gasoline demand is explored in Carol A. Dahl, "Gasoline Demand Survey," *The Energy Journal,* vol. 7, no. 1 (January 1986), pp. 67-82, and in DRI/McGraw-Hill, *An Analysis of Public Policy Measures to Reduce Carbon Dioxide Emission from the U.S. Transportation Sector,* chapter IV (Lexington, Mass.: DRI/McGraw Hill, January 1991) (prepared for the Office of Policy, Planning, and Evaluation, U.S. Environmental Protection Agency).

The Department of Energy studied the impact of a variety of energy taxes, including $0.50 per gallon, in U.S. Department of

Energy, Energy Information Administration, *Studies of Energy Taxes* (Washington, D.C.: DOE, April 1991).

One study found that gasoline taxes would need to rise by $0.45 per gallon (in nominal dollars) by the year 2000 and by $1.30 per gallon (in nominal dollars) by 2010 to stabilize carbon dioxide emissions from the U.S. light-duty fleet. See Roger E. Brinner et al., "Optimizing Tax Strategies to Reduce Greenhouse Gases Without Curtailing Growth," *Energy Journal*, vol. 12, no. 4 (Weston, Mass.: Gunn and Hain, 1991), pp. 1-14.

Revenue recycling is discussed in Roger E. Brinner et al., "Optimizing Tax Strategies to Reduce Greenhouse Gases without Curtailing Growth," *Energy Journal*, vol. 12, no. 4 (Weston, Mass.: Gunn and Hain, 1991), pp. 1-14.

A $1/gallon gasoline tax would have raised the average price of gasoline in 1990 in real terms from $0.92 to $1.68 (in 1982 dollars), the approximate price of premium unleaded gasoline in 1981. See U.S. Department of Energy, Energy Information Administration, *Studies of Energy Taxes* (Washington, D.C.: DOE, April 1991).

Issues associated with using a carbon tax to reduce emissions are discussed in Roger C. Dower and Mary Beth Zimmerman, *The Right Climate for Carbon Taxes: Creating Economic Incentives to Protect the Atmosphere* (Washington, D.C.: World Resources Institute, August 1992). The following chart demonstrates the various carbon content of some fossil fuels:

Carbon Content of Selected Fossil Fuels (in pounds).

Fuel	By Volume	By Energy Content (BTU*)
Coal	1440.00 (ton)	2.04
Crude oil	6.18 (gal)	1.60
Natural gas	0.03 (1000 ft3)	1.20
Gasoline	5.10 (gal)	1.50

* Units are represented as 10-4 lbs of CO_2 per BTU.

Source: Roger C. Dower and Robert Repetto, Testimony Before the Committee on Ways and Means, U.S. Congress (Washington, D.C., February 6, 1992), Table 2, "Carbon Content of Selected Fossil Fuels (lbs of carbon)."

Various carbon tax levels and their effects are explored in U.S. Department of Energy, Energy Information Administration, *Studies of Energy Taxes* (Washington, D.C.: DOE, April 1991); Congressional Budget Office, *Reducing the Deficit* (Washington, D.C.: CBO, February 1992); Congressional Budget Office, *Carbon Charges as a Response to Global Warming: The Effects of Taxing Fossil Fuels* (Washington, D.C.: CBO, August 1990); Robert Shackleton, *The Efficiency Value of Carbon Tax Revenues* (draft) (Washington, D.C.: Environmental Protection Agency, Energy Policy Branch, March 27, 1992); DRI/McGraw-Hill, *Economic Effects of Using Carbon Taxes to Reduce Carbon Dioxide Emissions in Major OECD Countries* (prepared for the U.S. Department of Commerce) (Lexington, Mass.: DRI/McGraw-Hill, January 1992); and Bureau of National Affairs, "EC's Carbon Tax Plans," *International Environmental Reporter* (Washington, D.C.: Bureau of National Affairs, April 8, 1992), p. 185.

Possible Carbon Tax Based on $30/Ton

Year	$/ Ton Carbon	$/ Ton Coal	$/ Barrel Oil	$/ 1000 ft.[3] Gas	Annual Revenues Billion $
1	6	3.60	0.77	0.10	7
2	12	7.20	1.54	0.19	14
3	18	10.80	2.31	0.30	21
4	24	14.40	3.09	0.40	28
5	30	18.00	3.85	0.48	36

Source: Roger C. Dower and Mary Beth Zimmerman, *The Right Climate for Carbon Taxes: Creating Economic Incentives to Protect the Atmosphere* (Washington, D.C.: World Resources Institute, August 1992), Table 2, "Proposed Carbon Tax Schedule of H.R. 1086." Schedule is roughly based on a study by the Congressional Budget Office and has been adjusted for inflation.

Water subsidies are discussed further in Marc Reisner and Sarah Bates, *Overtapped Oasis: Reform or Revolution for Western Water* (Washington, D.C.: Island Press, 1990); R.W. Wahl, *Markets for Federal Water: Subsidies, Property Rights, and the Bureau of Reclamation* (Washington, D.C.: Resources for the Future, 1989); House Subcommittee on General Oversight and Investigations, Committee on Interior and Insular Affairs, "Department of the Interior's Efforts to

Estimate the Cost of Federal Irrigation Subsidies: A Record of Deceit" (Washington, D.C.: U.S. Government Printing Office, 1988); Kenneth D. Frederick and James C. Hanson, *Water for Western Agriculture* (Washington, D.C.: Resources for the Future, 1982); and Bruce Babbitt, "Age-Old Challenge: Water and the West," *National Geographic* (June 1991), pp. 2-34.

The consumption of fresh water through irrigation and the provision of subsidized water by the Bureau of Reclamation is discussed in Richard W. Wahl, *Markets for Federal Water: Subsidies, Property Rights, and the Bureau of Reclamation* (Washington, D.C.: Resources for the Future, 1989); and Mohamed T. El-Ashry and Diana C. Gibbons, "The West in Profile," in Mohamed T. El-Ashry and Diana C. Gibbons, eds., *Water and Arid Lands of the Western United States* (New York, N.Y.: Cambridge University Press and World Resources Institute, 1988).

For more information on the environmental consequences of water diversion, see M. Reisner and Sarah Bates, *Overtapped Oasis: Reform or Revolution for Western Water* (Washington, D.C.: Island Press, 1990); Mohamed T. El-Ashry and Diana C. Gibbons, "The West in Profile," in Mohamed T. El-Ashry and Diana C. Gibbons, eds., *Water and Arid Lands of the Western United States* (New York, N.Y.: Cambridge University Press and World Resources Institute, 1988); and N. Hundley, Jr., "The Great American Desert Transformed: Aridity, Exploitation, and Imperialism in the Making of the Modern American West," in Mohamed T. El-Ashry and Diana C. Gibbons, eds., *Water and Arid Lands of the Western United States* (New York, N.Y.: Cambridge University Press and World Resources Institute, 1988).

Water markets are discussed in R.D. Hof, "California's Next Cash Crop May Soon Be . . . Water?" *Business Week* (March 2, 1992), pp. 76-78; and Richard W. Wahl, *Markets for Federal Water: Subsidies, Property Rights, and the Bureau of Reclamation* (Washington, D.C.: Resources for the Future, 1989).

Measurement of Economic Activity

For information about modifying prices to reflect environmental values, see Frances Cairncross, *Costing the Earth: The Challenges for Governments, the Opportunities for Business* (Cambridge, Mass.: Harvard Business School Press, 1992).

For a more complete discussion of the incorporation of environmental measures into national accounts, see United Nations Department of International Economic and Social Affairs, "Accounting for Sustainable Development," Working Paper 8 (New York, N.Y.: UN, 1987).

Information in the box on incorporating natural resources into national accounts can be found in Raul Solorzano et al., *Accounts Overdue: Natural Resource Depreciation in Costa Rica* (Washington, D.C.: World Resources Institute and San José, Costa Rica: Tropical Science Center, 1991); and Robert Repetto et al., *Wasting Assets: Natural Resources in the National Income Accounts* (Washington, D.C.: World Resources Institute, 1989).

For additional information on natural resource and environmental accounting, see Henry M. Peskin, *A Survey of Resource and Environmental Accounting in Industrialized Countries* (Washington, D.C.: World Bank, 1990); Robert Goodland, Herman Daly, and Salah El Serafy, eds., "Environmentally Sustainable Economic Development: Building on Brundtland," Environment Working Paper no. 46 (Washington, D.C.: World Bank, 1991); Organization for Economic Cooperation and Development, *Environmental Indicators: A Preliminary Set* (Paris: OECD, 1991); and Robert Repetto, "Earth in the Balance Sheet: Incorporating Natural Resources into National Income Accounts," *Environment* (September 1992), p. 12.

CHAPTER 4: ENVIRONMENTAL LITERACY

Education and Information

The notion that an environmentally literate society must build environmental values into economic development to sustain U.S. interests over the long haul is more thoroughly discussed in David W. Orr, *Ecological Literacy: Education and the Transition to a Postmodern World* (Albany, N.Y.: State University of New York Press, 1992).

For more information on the American Association for the Advancement of Science's Project 2061, see F. James Rutherford and Andrew Ahlgren, *Science for All Americans* (New York, N.Y.: Oxford University Press, 1989).

The information in the box on state environmental education programs is from U.S. Environmental Protection Agency, Office of Environmental Education, *Summary of the State Environmental Education Initiatives* (Washington, D.C.: EPA, 1992); and from literature provided by each state's education agency.

Leadership

For a closer look at environmental nongovernmental organizations, see Riley E. Dunlap and Angela G. Mertig, eds., *American Environmentalism: The U.S. Environmental Movement, 1970-1990* (New York, N.Y.: Taylor and Francis, 1992).

Information in the box on business initiatives for the environment can be found in Bruce Smart, ed., *Beyond Compliance: A New Industry View of the Environment* (Washington, D.C.: World Resources Institute, 1992); Stephan Schmidheiny with the Business Council for Sustainable Development, *Changing Course* (Cambridge, Mass.: Massachusetts Institute of Technology Press, 1992); and from the organizations named.

Public Participation and Civic Responsibility

Information on providing corporations with incentives to reduce pollution and increase product safety is found in "What Shareholders Really Want," *The New York Times*, Forum section, April 28, 1991.

CHAPTER 5: GOVERNANCE FOR SUSTAINABLE DEVELOPMENT

Integration of Environment with Other Policies

The excerpt from the Single European Act of 1987 comes from Title VII, Article 130r, Paragraph 2.

The problems associated with determining the adverse environmental effects of energy use are discussed in Susan Owens and C.W. Hope, "Energy and Environment: The Challenge of Integrating European Policies," *Energy Policy* (April 1987).

Information in the box on the Dutch plan can be found in *Environmental Program of the Netherlands: 1986-1990* (The Hague: SDU, 1986); Ir. F. Langeweg, ed., *Concern for Tomorrow: A National Environmental Survey 1985-2010* (Bilthoven: National Institute of Public Health and Environmental Protection, 1989); *To Choose or to Lose: National Environmental Policy Plan* (The Hague: SDU, 1989); and *National Environmental Policy Plan Plus* (The Hague: Ministry of Housing, Physical Planning and Environment, 1990).

More information on restructuring the President's Council on Environmental Quality can be found in Carnegie Commission on Science, Technology, and Government, *Environmental Research and Development:*

Strengthening the Federal Infrastructure (New York, N.Y.: Carnegie Commission on Science, Technology, and Government, December 1992).

The Erosion of Trust

Public opinion statistics were provided by the University of Michigan Center for Political Studies, Election Studies Division.

For further reading on the connection between trust and the ability to sustain democratic government, see Ronald Inglehart, "The Renaissance of Political Culture," *American Political Science Review*, vol. 82 (December 1988), pp. 1203-30.

An analysis of how the U.S. Environmental Protection Agency has been given restrictive and demanding laws to enforce while being deprived of necessary budgetary resources can be found in Richard J. Lazarus, "The Neglected Question of Congressional Oversight at EPA: Quis Custodiet Ipsos Custodes (Who Shall Watch the Watchers Themselves)," *Law and Contemporary Problems*, vol. 54, no. 205 (Durham, N.C.: Duke University School of Law, 1991), and Richard J. Lazarus, "The Tragedy of Distrust in the Implementation of Federal Environmental Law," *Law and Contemporary Problems*, vol. 54, no. 311 (Durham, N.C.: Duke University School of Law, 1991).

The state task force findings on pollution from federal facilities are found in the National Governors' Association and National Association of Attorneys General, Report of the Task Force on Federal Facilities, "From Crisis to Commitment: Environmental Cleanup and Compliance at Federal Facilities" (Washington, D.C.: National Governors' Association and National Association of Attorneys General, 1990).

Estimates on the costs of cleanup for the U.S. Department of Defense and Department of Energy facilities can be found in Congressional Budget Office, "Federal Liabilities Under Hazardous Waste Laws" (Washington, D.C.: CBO, April 1990), p. 47.

Openness and Equity

The EPA report summarizing the extent to which poor and minority groups suffer disproportionately from environmental problems in the United States is found in U.S. Environmental Protection Agency, *Environmental Equity: Reducing Risk for All Communities* (Washington, D.C.: EPA, June 1992). The major recommendations are as follows:

1. EPA should increase the priority that it gives to issues of environmental equity.

2. EPA should establish and maintain information that provides an objective basis for assessment of risks by income and race, beginning with developing a research and data collection plan.

3. EPA should incorporate considerations of environmental equity into the risk assessment process. It should revise its risk assessment procedures to ensure, where practical and relevant, better characterization of risk across populations, communities, or geographical areas. These revisions could be useful in determining whether there are any population groups at disproportionately high risk.

4. EPA should identify and target opportunities to reduce high concentrations of risk to specific population groups, employing approaches developed for geographic targeting.

5. EPA should, where appropriate, assess and consider the distribution of projected risk reduction in major rulemakings and Agency initiatives.

6. EPA should selectively review and revise its permit, grant, monitoring, and enforcement procedures to address high concentrations of risk in racial minority and low-income communities. Since state and local governments have primary authority for many environmental programs, EPA should emphasize to them its concerns about environmental equity.

7. EPA should expand and improve the level and forms with which it communicates with racial minority and low-income communities and should increase efforts to involve these communities in environmental policymaking.

8. EPA should establish mechanisms to ensure that environmental equity concerns are incorporated into its long-term planning and operations.

Race as a factor in hazardous waste facility siting practices is analyzed in Commission for Racial Justice, *Toxic Wastes and Race in the United States: A National Report on the Racial and Socio-Economic*

Characteristics of Communities with Hazardous Waste Sites (New York, N.Y.: United Church of Christ, 1990); and C. Lee, "Toxic Waste and Race in the United States," in Bunyan Bryant and Paul Mohai, eds., *Race and the Incidence of Environmental Hazards* (Boulder, Col.: Westview Press, 1992).

Information on the siting of landfills in the southeastern United States is drawn from the U.S. General Accounting Office, *Siting of Hazardous Waste Landfills and Their Correlation with Racial and Economic Status of Surrounding Communities* (Washington, D.C.: General Accounting Office, 1983).

A discussion of the distributional effects of environmental policies is found in Richard J. Lazarus, "Pursuing Environmental Justice: The Distributional Effects of Environmental Protection," *Northwestern University Law Review*, vol. 87 (March 1993) p.3.

Disparate enforcement and penalties of environmental laws were reported in "Unequal Protection: A Racial Divide in Environmental Law," *The National Law Journal*, vol. 15, no. 3 (New York, N.Y.: The New York Law Publishing Co., September 14, 1992), pp. S1-S12.

Hazardous waste siting in rural areas was analyzed by Clean Sites, Inc., *Hazardous Waste Sites and the Rural Poor: A Preliminary Assessment* (Alexandria, Va.: Clean Sites, Inc., March 1990).

Nicholas A. Ashford and Claudia S. Miller provide evidence that workplace standards for toxics are consistently and unjustifiably more lax than similar standards for the general population in *Chemical Exposures: Low Levels and High Stakes* (New York, N.Y.: Van Nostrand Reinhold, 1991).

CHAPTER 6: AMERICA'S NEW GLOBAL ROLE

The observation by George F. Kennan can be found in "Morality and Foreign Policy," *Foreign Affairs*, vol. 22 (Winter 1985-86), pp. 205-218.

Protecting the Global Environment

For discussions of global environmental issues, see the extensive presentations in World Resource Institute's *World Resources* series and the Worldwatch Institute's *State of the World* series. Also, see Cheryl Simon Silver and Ruth S. DeFries, *One Earth, One Future: Our Changing Global Environment* (Washington, D.C.: National Academy

Press, 1992); Anthony B. Wolbarst, ed., *Environment in Peril* (Washington, D.C.: Smithsonian Institution Press, 1991); Albert Gore, *Earth in the Balance: Healing the Global Environment* (Boston, Mass.: Houghton Mifflin, 1992); B.L. Turner II, ed., *The Earth as Transformed by Human Action: Global and Regional Changes in the Biosphere over the Past 300 Years* (New York, N.Y.: Cambridge University Press, 1991); and James Gustave Speth, "Environmental Pollution," in *Earth '88: Changing Geographic Perspectives* (Washington, D.C.: National Geographic Society, 1988), pp. 262-81; in addition to other articles in *Earth '88: Changing Geographic Perspectives* (Washington, D.C.: National Geographic Society, 1988).

Statistics on global problems are found in World Resources Institute, *World Resources 1992-93* (Washington, D.C.: World Resources Institute, 1992).

The need and opportunity for a new post-Cold War concept of national security for the United States is discussed by Jessica Tuchman Mathews in "Redefining Security," *Foreign Affairs*, vol. 68 (Spring 1989), p. 162.

The reference to the United States playing "a low-key defensive game" in its preparations and at negotiations during the Rio Earth Summit is from William K. Reilly in an EPA Agency-wide Memorandum, July 15, 1992, as reproduced in *Inside EPA* (August 7, 1992), pp. 6-7.

International Agreements and Institutions

A discussion of the need for new U.S. policies regarding developing countries is discussed by James Gustave Speth in "A Post-Rio Compact," *Foreign Policy*, vol. 88 (Fall 1992), pp. 145-161. For more information on international environmental treaties and institutions, see Lee A. Kimball, *Forging International Agreement: Strengthening Inter-Governmental Institutions for Environment and Development* (Washington, D.C.: World Resources Institute, April 1992).

Cooperation for Sustainable Development Abroad

For more detailed recommendations on how the United States can help developing countries achieve sustainable development, see Environmental and Energy Study Institute Task Force on International Development and Environmental Security, *Partnership for Sustainable*

Development: A New U.S. Agenda for International Development and Environmental Security (Washington, D.C.: EESI, 1991); Ralph H. Smuckler, and Robert J. Berg, *New Challenges, New Opportunities* (Washington, D.C.: World Resources Institute, 1988); Environment and Energy Study Institute Task Force on International Development and Environmental Security, *Partnership for Sustainable Development: A New U.S. Agenda for International Development and Environmental Security* (Washington, D.C.: EESI, 1991); and the Overseas Development Council, *Challenges and Priorities in the 1990s* (Washington, D.C.: ODC, 1992).

For more information on U.S. overseas development assistance, see Alexander R. Love, ed., *Development Assistance Efforts and Policies of the Members of the Development Assistance Committee, 1991 Report* (Paris: Organization for Economic Cooperation and Development, 1991).

The Schmidt Commission called for a combined doubling of development assistance from all Organization for Economic Cooperation and Development countries in *Facing One World,* a report by an independent group on financial flows to developing countries (Vienna, Austria: InterAction Council of Former Heads of Government, June 1989), p. 16.

For more information on an international system of regional centers to encourage appropriate technologies, see *International Environmental Research and Assessment: Proposals for Better Organization and Decision-Making* (New York, N.Y.: Carnegie Commission on Science, Technology, and Government, July 1992); and the Bellagio Conference Statement, "Relatively Advanced Developing Country Focus for Technology Cooperation Related to Global Climate Change" (Bellagio, Italy: October 28-November 1, 1991).

Curbing Population Growth

Statistics on the world's population growth, its associated problems, and funding needs were drawn from United Nations Population Fund (UNFPA), *The State of World Population 1990 and 1991* (New York: UNFPA, 1990, 1991); Robert Repetto, "Pollution, Resources, Environment: An Uncertain Future," *Population Bulletin,* vol. 42 (Washington, D.C.: Population Reference Bureau, 1987); "Population Growth and Conservation," *World Wildlife Fund and The Conservation Foundation Letter,* vol. 2 (Washington, D.C.: World Wildlife Fund and

The Conservation Foundation, 1990); United Nations Development Program, *Human Development Report 1991* (New York, N.Y.: Oxford University Press, 1991), p. 23; *World Development Report* (Washington, D.C.: World Bank, 1984); Environment and Energy Study Institute Task Force on International Development and Environmental Security, *Partnership for Sustainable Development* (Washington, D.C.: EESI, 1991); National Audubon Society and the Population Crisis Committee, *Why Population Matters* (New York, N.Y.: National Audubon Society, 1991); and Shanti R. Conly, J. Joseph Speidel, and Sharon L. Camp, *U.S. Population Assistance: Issues for the 1990s* (Washington, D.C.: Population Crisis Committee, 1991).

Integrating Trade and Environment

The original lawsuit raised both NAFTA and GATT claims (*Public Citizen et al. v. Office of the U.S. Trade Representative et al.*, [Civil Action 91-1916-D.D.C.] filed August 1, 1991, and Appeal 971 F. 2d 916 [D.C. Cir. 1992]) and was dismissed for lack of ripeness. After the United States agreed to NAFTA in September 1992, the plaintiffs refiled with respect only to NAFTA claims (Civil Action 92-2102-CRR, D.D.C., [filed September 15, 1992]).

The op-ed column on the difficulties of protecting free trade and the environment was written by Jessica Tuchman Mathews, "Dolphins, Tuna and Free Trade," *The Washington Post*, October 18, 1991.

Information in the box on the tuna/dolphin dispute can be found in U.S. Congress, Office of Technology Assessment, *Trade and Environment* (Washington, D.C.: U.S. Government Printing Office, May 1992).

The Council on Environmental Quality's *Environmental Quality: Twenty-first Annual Report* estimates that the worldwide market potentially available for U.S. exports of environmental goods and services is $60 billion (Washington, D.C.: U.S. Government Printing Office, 1990), p.xi.

For more information on U.S. companies that have relocated to Mexico to avoid U.S. occupational health laws, see U.S. General Accounting Office, "U.S.-Mexico Trade: Some U.S. Wood Furniture Firms Relocated from Los Angeles Area to Mexico" (Washington, D.C.: General Accounting Office, April 1991).

For a more detailed analysis of how environmental factors usually are outweighed by labor and transportation costs, taxes, and political stability in manufacturing location decisions, see H. Jeffrey Leonard, *Are Environmental Regulations Driving U.S. Industry Overseas?* (Washington, D.C.: The Conservation Foundation, 1984), and Christopher J. Duerksen, *Environmental Regulation of Industrial Plant Siting: How to Make It Work Better* (Washington, D.C.: The Conservation Foundation, 1983).

CHAPTER 7: ENERGY AND ENVIRONMENT

Sustainable Energy Strategies

According to the U.S. Department of Energy, fossil fuels provided nearly 88 percent of the world's energy in 1988. According to the Energy Information Administration, U.S. energy consumption by source (Quadrillion BTUs) was as follows in 1991:

Coal	Natural Gas	Petro- leum	Nuclear Electric Power	Hydro- Electric Power	Geo- thermal	Other	Total
18.81	20.16	32.72	6.54	3.08	0.17	0.03	81.51

Source: U.S. Department of Energy, Energy Information Administration, Office of Energy Markets and End Use, Annual Energy Review 1991 (Washington, D.C.: U.S. Department of Energy, 1992), Table 3.

Based on these figures, fossil fuels met approximately 90 percent of the U.S. energy demand. In addition, the United States relies heavily on petroleum imports to satisfy its demand for automotive fuels. In 1990, the United States imported 45 percent of its entire crude oil supply. Forty-three percent of the nation's refined petroleum products went toward gasoline for automobiles. See U.S. Department of Energy, Energy Information Administration, Office of Energy Markets and End Use, *Annual Energy Review 1989* (Washington, D.C.: DOE, 1989), Table 3 and p. 115, and *Annual Energy Review 1990* (Washington, D.C.: DOE, 1990), Table 3 and p. 115.

The Department of Energy's conservative estimates predict that energy consumption in the year 2030 will be 75 percent greater than in 1990. See U.S. Department of Energy, *National Energy Strategy: Powerful Ideas for America* (Washington, D.C.: DOE, February 1991), p. C-9.

The Role of Energy-Efficient Technologies

The U.S. Environmental Protection Agency's Green Lights program was initiated in 1991 and hopes to avoid up to $70 billion in utility-generating capacity. For more information on the program, see U.S. Environmental Protection Agency, Office of Air and Radiation, "Green Lights: A Voluntary Program to Prevent Pollution and Increase Competitiveness" (Washington, D.C.: EPA, December 1991). In addition, see U.S. Energy Association, *Getting Down to Business* (Boulder, Col.: RCG/Hagler, Bailly, 1992); Alliance to Save Energy, American Council for an Energy-efficient Economy, Natural Resources Defense Council, and Union of Concerned Scientists in consultation with the Tellus Institute America, *Energy Choices: Investing in a Strong Economy and a Clean Environment* (Cambridge, Mass.: Union of Concerned Scientists, 1992); and Alliance to Save Energy, American Gas Association, and Solar Energy Industries Association, *An Alternative Energy Future* (Washington, D.C.: Alliance to Save Energy, 1992).

The public hearings held during the development of the National Energy Strategy emphasized the need to place an increased emphasis on energy conservation and efficiency. See U.S. Department of Energy, *Interim Report: National Energy Strategy* (Washington, D.C.: DOE, April 1990), p. 4. Nevertheless, the National Energy Strategy placed more emphasis on energy supply than on efficiency. For instance, despite the acknowledged need to reduce oil imports, adopting the strategy would lead to a 60-percent increase over current levels by the year 2030. See James J. MacKenzie, *Toward a Sustainable Energy Future: The Critical Role of Rational Energy Pricing* (Washington, D.C.: World Resources Institute, May 1991).

For information on the potential of energy efficiency to minimize environmental degradation while meeting human needs and upholding quality of life, see Arnold P. Fickett, Clark W. Gellings, and Amory B. Lovins, "Efficient Use of Electricity," *Scientific American*, vol. 263, no. 3 (September 1990), pp. 64-74.

DOE funding for energy efficiency research and development has averaged less than 5 percent of all energy R&D funding. See U.S. Energy Association, *Getting Down to Business* (Washington, D.C.: USEA, 1992), p. 3. In addition, the USEA report provides various estimates of the potential energy saved through improved energy efficiency.

The average fuel efficiency of passenger cars has risen over the past

20 years. See U.S. Congress, Office of Technology Assessment, *Improving Automobile Fuel Economy: New Standards, New Approaches* (Washington, D.C.: U.S. Government Printing Office, October 1991), Table 4-1.

Between 1973 and 1986, U.S. consumption of primary energy and materials remained virtually unchanged, while during the same period the gross national product increased 35 percent. See Henry C. Kelly, "Energy Use and Productivity: Current Trends and Policy Implications" *Annual Reviews of Energy*, vol. 14 (Palo Alto, Calif.: Annual Reviews, 1989), pp. 321-53.

The Development of Advanced Energy Technologies

In the United States, there are over 1.2 million buildings with solar water heaters, approximately 250,000 pools with solar heating, and approximately 10,000 photovoltaic systems. See Solar Energy Industry Association, *Consumer Guide to Solar Energy* (Washington, D.C.: SEIA, 1991), p. 5; and Christopher Flavin and Rick Piltz, *Sustainable Energy* (Washington, D.C.: Renew America, 1989), p. 28.

Only 7 percent of the $2.7 billion fiscal year 1990 national budget for energy technology R&D was earmarked for conservation and efficiency.

Since 1980, federal funding for energy R&D has fallen rapidly. Despite modest increases under the Bush administration, the 1990 combined energy technology R&D budgets (in constant dollars) were still less than half of what they were in 1980. See U.S. Congress, Office of Technology Assessment, *Changing by Degrees: Steps to Reduce Greenhouse Gases* (Washington, D.C.: U.S. Government Printing Office, 1991).

In constant 1992 dollars, federal support for energy efficiency dropped from $949 million in FY1980 to $100 million in FY1988. In addition, federal support for renewable energy dropped from $1.1 billion in FY1980 to $102 million in FY1988. See Howard Wolpe's statement regarding budget priority setting at the Department of Energy, in U.S. House of Representatives, Committee on Science, Space and Technology, Subcommittee on Investigations and Oversight (May 19, 1992).

For more information on energy research and development, see American Association for the Advancement of Science, *Research and*

Development FY1991 (Washington, D.C.: AAAS, 1991). Also, see Solar Energy Research Institute, Idaho National Engineering Lab, Los Alamos National Lab, Oak Ridge National Lab, and Sandia National Labs, *The Potential of Renewable Energy* (Golden, Col., 1990).

On the transition to solar hydrogen, see Joan M. Ogden and Robert H. Williams, "Solar Hydrogen: Moving Beyond Fossil Fuels" (Washington, D.C.: World Resources Institute, October 1989).

Moving Onto a Sustainable Development Path

The use of renewable resources to generate electricity within a state is related more to the regulatory policies and practices of the state utility commission than to the actual availability of renewable resources. See David H. Moskowitz, "Cutting the Nation's Electric Bill," *Issues in Science and Technology*, vol. 5 (Spring 1989), pp. 88-93.

CHAPTER 8: PREVENTING POLLUTION

Integration of Pollution Control Functions

For more information on problems with the existing pollution control system, see National Academy of Public Administration, *Steps Toward a Stable Future: A Report* (Washington, D.C.: NAPA, 1984); and Joseph L. Sax, "Environmental Law in the Law Schools: What We Teach and How We Feel About It," *Environmental Law Reporter*, vol. 19 (1989), p. 10253.

For more information on how environmental risk can serve as the basis for budgeting, regulatory, and enforcement policies, see U.S. Environmental Protection Agency, Science Advisory Board, *Reducing Risk: Setting Priorities and Strategies for Environmental Protection* (Washington, D.C.: EPA, September 1990); and U.S. Environmental Protection Agency, Office of Policy, Planning, and Evaluation, *Unfinished Business* (Washington, D.C.: EPA, February 1987).

For more information on cross-media approaches to pollution control, see "Integrated Pollution Control: A Symposium," *Environmental Law*, vol. 22 (1992), pp. 1-348; and Nigel Haigh and Frances Irwin, eds., *Integrated Pollution Control in Europe and North America* (Washington, D.C.: The Conservation Foundation, 1990).

For more information on the use of a systems approach to reduce pollutants in coal-fired power plants, see Electric Power Research Institute (EPRI), *Integrated Environmental Control for Coal-Fired Power*

Plants (New York, N.Y.: American Society of Mechanical Engineers [ASME], 1981); and EPRI, *Second Symposium on Integrated Environmental Control for Coal-Fired Power Plants* (New York, N.Y.: ASME, 1983).

The principal pollution prevention report of the Office of Technology Assessment is *Serious Reduction of Hazardous Waste: For Pollution Prevention and Industrial Efficiency* (Washington, D.C.: U.S. Government Printing Office, September 1986).

The passage from the Organization for Economic Cooperation and Development Council Act can be found in OECD's *Recommendation on Integrated Pollution Prevention and Control* [(90) 164 (Final)], adopted January 31, 1991.

On state initiatives in integrated environmental management, see Barry G. Rabe, *Fragmentation and Integration in State Environmental Management* (Washington, D.C.: The Conservation Foundation, 1986).

Information in the box on integration models was based on Graham Bennett and Konrad von Moltke, "Integrated Permitting in the Netherlands and the Federal Republic of Germany," and Don Hinrichsen, "Integrated Permitting and Inspection in Sweden," in Nigel Haigh and Frances Irwin, eds., *Integrated Pollution Control in Europe and North America* (Washington, D.C.: The Conservation Foundation, 1990).

See the Massachusetts Toxics Use Reduction Act, M.G.L. c.21i, Section 3 (D)(E), and Manik Roy and Lee A. Dillard, "Toxics Use Reduction in Massachusetts: The Blackstone Project," *Journal of the Air and Waste Management Association*, vol. 40 (1990), p. 1368.

Further information on The Conservation Foundation integrated pollution control statute can be obtained from Terry Davies, Resources for the Future, Washington, D.C.

Science and Priorities

The need to increase government research funds devoted to the environment is based on information in National Science Foundation, *Science and Engineering Indicators—1991* (Washington, D.C.: NSF, 1991).

For a closer look at the inverted priorities at EPA, see U.S. Environmental Protection Agency, Science Advisory Board, *Reducing Risk* (Washington, D.C.: EPA, September 1990).

On the differing roles of scientists and policymakers, see Gene E. Likens, *The Ecosystem Approach: Its Use and Abuse* (Oldendorf/Luhe, Germany: Ecology Institute, 1992).

For more information on the importance of risk communication in environmental decisionmaking, see Peter Sandman, "Getting to Maybe: Some Communications Aspects of Siting Hazardous Waste Facilities," and Paul Slovic, Baruch Fischoff, and Sarah Lichtenstein, "Rating the Risks," in Theodore S. Glickman and Michael Gough, eds., *Readings in Risk* (Washington, D.C.: Resources for the Future, 1990).

For more information on adverse health effects caused by environmental contaminants, see *Toxic Chemicals in the Great Lakes and Associated Effects* (Ottawa, Canada: Canada Department of Fisheries and Oceans, March 1991); and Theodora Colborn and Coralie Clement, eds., *Chemically Induced Alterations in Sexual and Functional Development: The Wildlife/Human Connection* (Princeton, N.J.: Princeton Scientific Publishers, 1992).

For a closer look at the problems associated with the depletion of the stratospheric ozone layer, see World Health Organization, *Scientific Assessment of Stratospheric Ozone* (Geneva: WHO, February 1991); and United Nations, *Environmental Effects of Ozone Depletion—1991* (Nairobi, Kenya: UNEP, 1991).

The conflicts between environmental scientists and health scientists are discussed in Gilbert S. Omenn, "Forum Two: Do We Know Enough to Take a Risk-Based Approach?" *EPA Journal*, vol. 17 (March/April 1991), p. 33.

For a good example of a risk assessment paradigm, see *Improving Aquatic Risk Assessment under FIFRA* (Washington, D.C.: Resolve, 1992).

"Science, as my position has really made clear to me, is really all we have." See William K. Reilly, Remarks to World Wildlife Fund Board of Directors, Tucson, Arizona, February 12, 1991, p. 5.

An example of a report with goal-setting and measurable objectives can be found in U.S. Department of Health and Human Services, Public Health Service, *Healthy People 2000: National Health Promotion and Disease Prevention Objectives* (Washington, D.C.: U.S. Government Printing Office, 1990).

Land Use

More than 90 percent of the original forests have been lost since
the first Europeans settled in the United States. See *World Wildlife
Fund Atlas of the Environment* (New York, N.Y.: Prentice Hall, 1990);
and Worldwatch Institute, *State of the World* (New York, N.Y.: W.W.
Norton & Co., 1992).

Ninety-nine percent of the tall-grass prairies have been lost. See
World Resources Institute, *World Resources 1990-91* (Washington,
D.C.: World Resources Institute, 1991), p. 126.

Fewer than 6 percent of the original 215 million acres of wetlands
remain. See Thomas E. Dahl and Craig E. Johnson, *Status and Trends
in the Coterminous United States: Mid 1970s to Mid 1980s*
(Washington, D.C.: U.S. Department of the Interior, Fish and Wildlife
Service, 1991).

Wetlands continue to be lost at a rate of roughly 300,000 acres
per year. See U.S. Environmental Protection Agency, *Natural Resources
of the 21st Century: An Evaluation of the Effects of Land Use on
Environmental Quality* (Washington, D.C.: EPA, 1985), p. 32; and
U.S. Environmental Protection Agency, Office of Wetlands Protection,
Wetlands Action Plan (Washington, D.C.: EPA, 1989).

Approximately 500 plant and animal species are known to have
become extinct in the United States since Europeans arrived. See
Council on Environmental Quality, *Environmental Quality: 21st
Annual Report* (Washington, D.C.: CEQ, 1990).

Statement on U.S. urban development is taken from Charles N.
Glaab and A. Theodore Brown, *A History of Urban America* (New
York, N.Y.: Macmillan, 1967), p. 7.

For a general overview of the issues involved in U.S. land-use reg-
ulation, see Richard H. Jackson, *Land Use in America* (New York, N.Y.:
John Wiley, 1981); and Elaine Moss, ed., *Land Use Controls in the
United States* (New York, N.Y.: Dial Press, 1977) (for the Natural
Resources Defense Council).

The most recent Supreme Court statement on land-use regulation
to protect the environment is its decision in *Lucas v. South Carolina
Coastal Council,* 60 U.S.L.W. 4842 (S.Ct., June 29, 1992).

The National Land Use Policy Act originally was proposed by the Nixon administration in 1971. The act would have created a program establishing land-use guidelines and authorized the granting of federal funds to states as an incentive to develop state land-use programs protecting areas of critical environmental concern. Drawing from this proposal and a bill introduced by Senator Henry M. Jackson, the Land Use Policy Planning and Assistance Act of 1972 passed the Senate but failed to pass the House of Representatives.

For a more detailed analysis of federal land-use policy proposals, see William K. Reilly, "New Directions in Federal Land Use Regulation," in David Listokin, ed., *Land Use Controls: Present Problems and Future Reform* (New Brunswick, N.J.: Center for Urban Policy Research, 1974).

Information in the box on the Coastal Zone Management Act was provided by David G. Godschalk, "Implementing Coastal Zone Management: 1972-1990," *Coastal Management*, vol. 20 (April-June 1992), pp. 93-116; and David W. Owens, "National Goals, State Flexibility, and Accountability in Coastal Zone Management," *Coastal Management*, vol. 20 (April-June 1992), pp. 143-65; and from the Office of Coastal and Resource Management, National Oceanic and Atmospheric Administration, Washington, D.C.

Federal Lands

Information on federal timber sales and their costs and revenues are discussed in U.S. Department of Agriculture, Forest Service, *Timber Sale Program Annual Report, FY1988, Forest Level Information* (Washington, D.C.: U.S. Government Printing Office, 1989); Congressional Budget Office, *Reducing the Deficit* (Washington, D.C.: U.S. Congress, February 1992); P.M. Emerson, "The Below Cost Timber Sale Issue: Going Against the Grain?" *Western Wildlands*, vol. 12 (Spring 1986), pp. 16-21; M.A. Francis, Testimony Before the Subcommittee on Forests, Family Farms, and Energy, U.S. House of Representatives (Washington, D.C., October 30, 1991); and Richard E. Rice, *National Forests—Policies for the Future, Vol. 5: The Uncounted Costs of Logging* (Washington, D.C.: The Wilderness Society, 1989).

For more information on the environmental problems associated with current logging practices, see Richard E. Rice, "Old Growth Logging Myths: The Ecological Impact of the U.S. Forest Service's

Management Policies," *The Ecologist*, vol. 20, no. 4 (1990), pp. 141-45; and Alice M. Rivlin, Testimony Before the Budget Committee, U.S. Senate (Washington, D.C., March 15, 1989).

Legislation to repeal the 1872 Mining Act was pending before Congress as of the time this report went to press. For more information on the history of the 1872 Mining Act, see John D. Leshy, *The Mining Law* (Washington, D.C.: Resources for the Future, 1987); U.S. Congress, Office of Technology Assessment, *Management of Nonfuel Minerals in Federal Land* (Washington, D.C.: U.S. Government Printing Office, 1979); The Wilderness Society, *New Directions for the Forest Service* (Alexandria, Va.: Global Printing, 1989); and The Wilderness Society, Statement of Dr. W. Thomas Georold before the Subcommittee on Mineral Resource Development and Production, Energy and Natural Resources Committee, U.S. Senate (Washington, D.C., September 13, 1990).

Information on grazing fees on public lands was derived from Alice M. Rivlin, statement before the Budget Committee, U.S. Senate (Washington, D.C., March 15, 1989); and Congressional Budget Office, *Reducing the Deficit* (Washington, D.C.: CBO, 1991).

Protecting Biodiversity

For an overview of the problems facing biodiversity conservation, see Paul Ehrlich and Edward O. Wilson, "Biodiversity Studies: Science and Policy," *Science*, vol. 253 (August 16, 1991), pp. 758-62; Walter V.C. Reid and Kenton R. Miller, *Keeping Options Alive: The Scientific Basis for Conserving Biodiversity* (Washington, D.C.: World Resources Institute, 1989); Edward O. Wilson, "Threats to Biodiversity," *Scientific American* (September 1989), pp. 108-14; Council on Environmental Quality, *Environmental Quality: 21st Annual Report* (Washington, D.C.: CEQ, 1990); and Edward O. Wilson, *The Diversity of Life* (Cambridge, Mass.: Harvard University Press, 1992).

For more information on protecting biodiversity with EPA's existing authority, see Robert L. Fishman, *Biological Diversity and Environmental Protection: Authorities to Reduce Risk* (Washington, D.C.: Environmental Law Institute, 1991).

For more information on the increase in ultraviolet radiation resulting from the thinning of the ozone layer, see R.C. Smith, "Ozone Depletion: Ultraviolet Radiation and Phytoplankton Biology in

Antarctic Waters," *Science,* vol. 254 (February 21, 1992); United Nations Environment Programme, "Environmental Effects of Ozone Depletion: 1991 Update," Panel Report Pursuant to Article 6 of the Montreal Protocol on Substances that Deplete the Ozone Layer" (Nairobi, Kenya: UNEP, 1991); and R.C. Worrest, "Impact of Solar Ultraviolet-B Radiation (290-320 nm) Upon Marine Microalgae," *Physiologia Plantarum,* vol. 58 (Copenhagen, Denmark: Munksgaard International Publishers, 1983), pp. 428-34.

At the state level, California's Memorandum of Understanding provides a model for coordinating land management to protect biodiversity. It represents the first time that a state and the federal government have agreed to work cooperatively in conserving biodiversity on a regional basis across administrative boundaries. For more information, see "Bioregional Strategy Adopted for Resource Conservation," press release from the Resources Agency, State of California, September 19, 1991; and California Council on Biodiversity, "Memorandum of Understanding: California's Coordinated Regional Strategy to Conserve Biological Diversity" (Sacramento, Cal., September 19, 1991).

For more information on the impacts of the Endangered Species Act, see Michael J. Bean, Sarah G. Fitzgerald, and Michael A. O'Connell, *Reconciling Conflicts Under the Endangered Species Act: The Habitat Conservation Planning Experience* (Washington, D.C.: World Wildlife Fund, 1991); Walter V.C. Reid, "The U.S. Needs a National Biodiversity Policy" (Washington, D.C.: World Resources Institute, February 1992); and M. Rupert Cutler, "Meeting the Biodiversity Challenge Through Coordinated Land-Use Planning," *Renewable Resources Journal,* vol. 9 (Winter 1991), pp. 13-16.

For information on a global biodiversity strategy, see World Resources Institute, The World Conservation Union, and United Nations Environment Programme, in consultation with the Food and Agriculture Organization and the United Nations Education, Scientific, and Cultural Organization, *Global Biodiversity Strategy: Guidelines for Action to Save, Study, and Use the Earth's Biotic Wealth Sustainably and Equitably* (Washington, D.C.: World Resources Institute; Gland, Switzerland: The World Conservation Union; and Nairobi, Kenya: UNEP, 1992).

Information in the box on gap analysis was provided by

Defenders of Wildlife, *National Biodiversity Inventory: Appropriations Request and Background Information* (Washington, D.C.: Defenders of Wildlife, 1991); J. Michael Scott et al., *Gap Analysis: Protecting Biodiversity Using Geographical Information Systems* handbook prepared for a workshop held at the University of Idaho, October 29-30, 1990; and Keith Schneider, "Prospecting for Habitat: How to Map Out the Best Places for Rare Species," *New York Times*, Week in Review section, June 3, 1990, p. 5.

The plight of the coral reefs is described in "Coral Reefs Off 20 Countries Face Assaults from Man and Nature," *New York Times*, March 27, 1990, p. C4.

CHOOSING A SUSTAINABLE FUTURE

ACKNOWLEDGMENTS

The Commission is indebted to many people and organizations who contributed to the production of this report. Preeminent among them are J. Clarence (Terry) Davies, the Commission's executive director, and Amelia Salzman, its project director. They were ably supported by the rest of the Commission staff: Wendy Laird, John Roach, and Amy Townsend, research fellows; Will Allen, research assistant; Linda Durkee, a consultant who helped write and edit sections of the report; and Gwendolyn C. Harley, commission assistant/executive secretary. Nancy Hopps and Fredline Jean-Baptiste graciously provided additional staff assistance. Catherine Williams deserves special thanks for keeping the Chairman on track during this project.

World Wildlife Fund (WWF), which convened and supported the Commission,[1] and particularly its President, Kathryn S. Fuller, who was enthusiastic about the project from its inception, deserve our deep appreciation.

Several experts made presentations and participated in the Commission's discussions on subjects of particular concern to the Commission. We are indebted to the following individuals for sharing their informative and provocative insights: Jesse H. Ausubel (Rockefeller University), Ambassador Richard Benedick, E.U. Curtis Bohlen (U.S. State Department), D. Allan Bromley (President's Office

---

[1] Unless otherwise indicated, the individuals we mention are World Wildlife Fund staff.

of Science and Technology), Anthony Cortese (Tufts University), Michael Mantell (California Department of Natural Resources), Jessica T. Mathews (World Resources Institute), William K. Reilly (U.S. Environmental Protection Agency), Robert Repetto (WRI), and Richard Schmalensee (Massachusetts Institute of Technology).

The Commission also benefited greatly from various briefing papers prepared by: Blair T. Bower, T.J. Glauthier, Frances H. Irwin, Richard J. Lazarus (Washington University School of Law), John Rosenberg (*Vermont* magazine), Mark Sagoff (University of Maryland), and Robert Smythe.

We appreciate the contributions of congressional and federal observers: Patty Beneke (Senate Committee on Energy and Natural Resources), David Clement (House Committee on Science, Space, and Technology), Jack Clough and Keith Cole (House Committee on Energy and Commerce), John Doyle (House Committee on Public Works and Transportation), Daniel Fiorino (U.S. EPA), Richard Grundy (Senate Committee on Energy and Natural Resources), Kate Kimball (Senate Committee on Environment and Public Works), Eileen Lee and Michael Rodemeyer (House Committee on Science, Space, and Technology), Tom Melius (House Committee on Merchant Marine and Fisheries), Jack Schenendorf (House Committee on Environment and Public Works), Raphaelle Semmes (Council on Environmental Quality), Steve Shimberg (Senate Committee on Environment and Public Works), and Will Stelle (House Committee on Merchant Marine and Fisheries, Subcommittee on Fisheries and Wildlife Conservation and the Environment).

Considerable credit is also due to those who critically reviewed drafts of our report: Munroe Newman of the Appalachian Regional Commission; Philip Shabecoff of Greenwire; Paul Portney of Resources for the Future; Roger Dower, Walter Reed, and Robert Repetto of World Resources Institute; and William Eichbaum and James P. Leape of World Wildlife Fund.

We would also like to acknowledge the participants in a round-table meeting convened in May 1990 to discuss whether to convene a National Commission on the Environment, and if so, to describe its agenda. In addition to several members of this Commission who attended that meeting, we would like to thank Robert Arnott (ERM–Rocky Mountain), Richard Carlson (Carlson, Knight and

Krudna), Anthony Cortese (Tufts University), Henry Diamond (Beveridge and Diamond), Anthony Earl (Quarrels and Brady), Kathy Fletcher (People for Puget Sound), A. Alan Hill (consultant), Russell Peterson (former CEQ Chairman), and John Sawhill (the Nature Conservancy) for their important contributions to this effort.

Candra Currie and Janet Fesler were extremely helpful in arranging the commission's many meetings and events.

The report was edited by Robert McCoy and Martha Cooley, a freelance editor. Cathleen Currier of World Resources Institute lent her editorial skills to the summary statement. Allison Rogers produced the report and provided editorial assistance. Fannie Mae Keller provided additional production assistance.

Barbara Rodes and Carla Langeveld provided essential research assistance, drawing our attention to and providing us with important reports and research documents throughout the process.

Finally, we are deeply grateful to The George Gund Foundation, The Johnson Foundation (and particularly Jon Vondracek for his support and helpful suggestions), The Joyce Foundation, The Summit Foundation, Richard King Mellon Foundation, and Howard Phipps Foundation, without whose generosity this undertaking would not have been possible.

BIOGRAPHICAL
SKETCHES OF
THE COMMISSIONERS

RUSSELL E. TRAIN (Chairman, National Commission on the Environment) is Chairman of World Wildlife Fund (WWF). Previously, he served as EPA Administrator and was the first Chairman of the President's Council on Environmental Quality, Under Secretary of the Department of the Interior, and Judge of the U.S. Tax Court.

PETER A.A. BERLE is President of the National Audubon Society. Previously, he was a partner with the law firm Berle, Kass & Case; headed the New York State Department of Environmental Conservation; and served three terms in the New York State Assembly. In 1989, Mr. Berle was appointed by Governor Mario Cuomo as Chairman of the special Commission on the Adirondacks in the 21st Century.

JOHN E. BRYSON is Chairman and Chief Executive officer of SCEcorp and Southern California Edison Company. Previously, he was a partner with the San Francisco law firm Morrison and Foerster. He served as President of the California Public Utilities Commission and Chairman of the California State Water Resources Control Board. He has also served as Vice Chairman of the Oregon Energy Facility Siting Council and was a co-founder of and attorney for the Natural Resources Defense Council.

A.W. CLAUSEN is a Director and Chairman of the Executive Committee of the Board of Directors for BankAmerica Corporation and its wholly owned subsidiary, Bank of America N.T.&S.A. Previously, he was Chairman and Chief Executive Officer of the Corporation and the Bank. He was President of The World Bank between 1981 and 1986.

DOUGLAS M. COSTLE is Distinguished Senior Fellow, Institute for Sustainable Communities. Previously, he was Dean of the Vermont Law School, EPA Administrator, Assistant Director of the Congressional Budget Office, Commissioner of the Connecticut Department of Environmental Protection, and Senior Staff Associate to the President's Advisory Council on Executive Organization (Ash Council).

MADELEINE MAY KUNIN is the former three-term Governor of Vermont. She is the President of the Institute for Sustainable Communities, a nonprofit environmental organization focused on Eastern and Central Europe. For the 1992 fall term, she is the first Nelson Rockefeller Center Distinguished Visiting Fellow in public policy at Dartmouth College. Last year she was the first public policy fellow at Radcliffe College, Harvard University.

GENE E. LIKENS is Vice President of The New York Botanical Garden and Director of the Institute of Ecosystem Studies. Concurrently, he holds faculty positions at Yale, Cornell, and Rutgers universities. Dr. Likens, an ecologist, has authored more than 300 scientific publications and has written or edited 10 books.

CRUZ A. MATOS is currently a consultant. Previously, he was United Nations Chief Technical Advisor to South Pacific developing countries following an assignment as Chief Technical Advisor to Caribbean developing countries. He served the government of Puerto Rico as Secretary for Natural Resources and was Director of the Environmental Quality Board. Prior to his international and government service, Mr. Matos was President and Chief Executive Officer of Fisher and Porter de Puerto Rico.

GILBERT S. OMENN is Professor of Medicine and Environmental Health and Dean of the School of Public Health and Community

Medicine, University of Washington, Seattle. He served as a deputy to Frank Press, President Carter's Science and Technology Adviser, and later as an Associate Director of the Office of Management and Budget. Dr. Omenn was a visiting Senior Fellow at Princeton's Woodrow Wilson School and the first Science and Public Policy Fellow at The Brookings Institution. He is author of 254 research papers and scientific reviews and author/editor of eight books.

PAUL H. O'NEILL is Director, Chairman of the Board, and Chief Executive Officer of Alcoa. Previously, he was President of International Paper Co. and served on the staff of the U.S. Office of Management and Budget.

ALICE M. RIVLIN is a Senior Fellow in the Economic Studies Program at The Brookings Institution. Previously, she was Director of the Economic Studies Program at Brookings; the first Director of the Congressional Budget Office; and Assistant Secretary of Planning and Evaluation at the U.S. Department of Health, Education, and Welfare. Dr. Rivlin received a MacArthur Foundation fellowship and was Godkin Lecturer at Harvard University. She is a past president of the American Economic Association. She chairs the Board of Trustees for The Wilderness Society and, in 1990 and 1991, chaired the Commission on Budget and Financial Priorities of the District of Columbia.

PRISCILLA ROBINSON is a consultant in Tucson, Arizona, providing services to clients in public affairs, community education, and administrative and legislative lobbying. Previously, she was Director of Southwest Environmental Service, a nonprofit environmental advocacy organization. While director, she played a major role in bringing Arizona smelters into compliance with legal requirements, served on the task force that wrote the Arizona Environmental Quality Act of 1986, and authored a citizen's handbook on the Clean Air Act titled *Blue Skies: An Arizona Guide to Clean Air.*

STEVEN C. ROCKEFELLER is Professor of Religion at Middlebury College in Vermont. Dr. Rockefeller is author of *John Dewey: Religious Faith and Democratic Humanism.* He is co-editor of *Spirit and Nature: Why the Environment is a Religious Issue.* He is also the Vice Chairman of the Rockefellers Brother Fund.

WILLIAM D. RUCKELSHAUS is Chairman and Chief Executive Officer of Browning-Ferris Industries, Inc. Previously, he was Senior Vice President of Weyerhaeuser Company, U.S. Representative to the United Nations World Commission on Environment and Development, two-time EPA Administrator, Deputy U.S. Attorney General, Acting Director of the Federal Bureau of Investigation, and Majority Leader for the Indiana House of Representatives.

GLORIA R. SCOTT is President of Bennett College. Previously, she was Vice President of Clark College. She has held teaching and administration positions at Knoxville College, North Carolina A&T State University, Texas Southern University, Bryn Mawr College, Clark College, and Grambling State University.

JAMES GUSTAVE SPETH is a founder and President of World Resources Institute. Previously, he served as Chairman of the President's Council on Environmental Quality and was professor of law at Georgetown University Law Center. He was a founder and senior attorney at Natural Resources Defense Council (NRDC) after serving as a law clerk for U.S. Supreme Court Justice Hugo L. Black.

LEE M. THOMAS is Chairman and Chief Executive Officer of Law Companies Environmental Group. Previously, he was EPA Administrator, Assistant Administrator for Solid Waste and Emergency Response of EPA, Executive Deputy Director of the Federal Emergency Management Agency, and Director of the Division of Public Safety Programs and Executive Director of the Office of Criminal Justice Programs for the Office of the Governor of South Carolina.

VICTORIA J. TSCHINKEL is a senior consultant for Landers and Parsons, attorneys at law. Previously, she was Secretary of Florida's Department of Environmental Regulation. She served on EPA's Acid Rain Advisory Committee and the National Academy of Sciences' Panel on the Policy Implications of Greenhouse Warming. Ms. Tschinkel has written numerous articles on environmental management.

ROBERT M. WHITE is President of the National Academy of Engineering and serves as Vice Chairman of the National Research Council. Previously, he was President of the University Corporation for Atmospheric Research and President of the Joint Oceanographic Institution; Chief of the U.S. Weather Bureau; and the first Administrator of the National Oceanic and Atmospheric Administration. Dr. White was the U.S. Commissioner on the International Whaling Commission and the U.S. representative to the World Meteorological Organization.

INDEX

F

G

L

M

N